Also by Albert Paul Messina

The Decline and Fall of Charity

Albert Paul Messina

The Nonprofit Leader as Liberal Thinker:

Politics, Ethics and Strategy Reconsidered

Philanthropy House Press

Printed in the United States of America

ISBN-10: 0983507538

ISBN-13: 9780983507536

To the memory of my mother

Catherine Ann Matson Messina
1932-2007

Who encouraged my curiosity

And my father

Albert C. Messina
1929-1988

Who wanted me to, as he put it, "push a pencil."
Which, in the writing of this book
and the curiosity that shaped it,
I did indeed push.

Contents

Prologue
The Good Life

What is thy art? To be good.
~Marcus Aurelius

Anyone who tries to be good all the time will come to ruin among the great many who are not good.
~Machiavelli

Friendship is rare. A childhood friendship that lasts into adulthood is rarer still. My friendship with Steve Steinman, who was the first to tell me that I ought to write a book about the political dimensions of nonprofits, is one of those rare relationships that extended deep into adulthood, now almost five full decades deep. Our many conversations about nonprofits confirmed for Steve—a business consultant educated at the Wharton School and the University of Chicago—that the political dimension of nonprofits, though largely ignored, needed to be written about and communicated to the millions of Americans who serve as the CEOs of the nation's nonprofits or serve as volunteers on their behalf. My conversations with Steve Steinman also taught me that the political and professional sides of life, important as they may be, are not as important as the larger context into which they are appropriately placed: the ethical dimension of a life lived well. I came to realize that Steve and I—Steve more so than I—had been reading broadly and deeply in the humanities since our undergraduate days in the late sixties and early seventies. In doing so—reading and discussing and reflecting on history and philosophy and literature and politics—we had arrived at a worldview that regarded career and commercial success as smaller ideas circumscribed by life's larger meaning.

But ultimately I made the decision to write **The Nonprofit Leader as Liberal Thinker** one afternoon as I sat in a conference room in the middle of Manhattan. I had been asked to serve on a committee to plan a conference for Youth Association International, a youth development organization whose mission is to enable young people from disadvantaged circumstances to become productive and engaged citizens. We were a committee of twenty-five: CEOs like myself of local Youth Association International organizations, board volunteers from local organizations, and international staffers from the office based in New York City. We were all seated at a large conference table in a spacious but windowless room in the Empire State Building.

The meeting had gone just like every other conference-planning meeting I previously attended: predictably well. We talked about the same subjects: board development and fundraising, marketing and communications, executive leadership and public trust; and we ultimately settled on a conference program not unlike the previous year's program, not unlike the conference program from the year before that, not unlike every other program I could remember from my more than twenty-five years of working for this venerable institution. Our conference planning, like the Youth Association International profession itself, like the wider world of nonprofit management, had become from my perspective vaudevillian in its redundance. It was the same act, the same topic, the same shtick conference after conference, leading me and my more experienced colleagues to miss many of the sessions at these conferences in favor of informal gatherings in hotel rooms and bars and restaurants.

I met Patrick McSweeney at one of these

informal gatherings, the man who became the foremost mentor in my professional career, a Boston-born and Jesuit-educated thinker with a penchant for organizational politics and a taste for single malt scotch. Although Patrick McSweeney was not at the conference planning meeting in Manhattan, somehow his spirit of loyal opposition was unexpectedly invoked when one of the national staffers observed, "None of this training, none of these conference sessions, not any single session, not all of them taken as a whole, not even the accumulation of them over a career, can really teach someone how to survive so they can succeed as a nonprofit CEO."

Over the years I had heard various versions of this survive-to-succeed idea from Patrick McSweeney as he held court late at night in the lounge of a hotel bar with a scotch in one hand and a cigar in the other. But Patrick, whose philosophical temperament tended to be nuanced, even obscure at times, had never put the problem of being a nonprofit CEO as succinctly and as astutely as our old friend and colleague Doug Hays had done. Doug Hays had grown up in the Youth Association organization in Binghamton, New York, started his Youth Association career in Chicago, but had spent most of his career working either in the USA Regional Office or as the CEO of one of the New Jersey Youth Association organizations. It always seemed to me that the Jersey experience had been the defining one for Doug Hays: he walked and talked like a world-weary wiseguy from Jersey, which, along with his loyalty to the autonomy of local Youth Association organizations, may have accounted for his being overlooked on every occasion for more senior supervisory positions in the international organization; and thus he remained, after more than thirty years in the field, in an entry-level position with the elevated but inconsequential title of Regional Service Director.

But Doug Hays's years of experience also taught him that success as a nonprofit CEO could come and go and that sustaining success or aspiring to it required a certain wisdom to survive, which in turn required a certain political acumen. His point at the Manhattan meeting was simply that training, even if it had the breadth, which it rarely if ever has, or the depth, which is rarer still, cannot adequately educate one to be a CEO of a nonprofit organization. Part of the reason training cannot adequately educate a CEO is that training, unlike education, imparts information; on occasion, knowledge, but never wisdom. It takes a political wisdom to survive and succeed as a nonprofit CEO, and the mastery of that political dimension cannot be found in nonprofit training programs, nor in non-profit literature.

The training experiences I encountered in my career, whether they were workshops that were days in duration or conference keynotes that lasted twenty minutes, always had one overriding assumption: that the people engaged on behalf of nonprofits—as board members, CEOs, staff, volunteers, donors, or funders—were all people of good will who could be counted upon to conduct themselves fairly, ethically, truthfully. This sanguine view of human nature was never stated explicitly in any training I ever encountered, but was implied by the fact that it was never addressed at all. At the very least, the professional training I received was neutral on the issue of human nature, which left me vulnerable to the machinations of people of ill will, to people who are petty, to people who nurse grievances, to people who lie and dissemble to gain an advantage. I never encountered a training session on how to handle staff members who go behind your back to the board, or a session on board members who have an eye on your position as CEO rather than on the mission and well-being of the institution. The sanguine view of human nature, which is prevalent in my field and perhaps prevalent in the nonprofit field in general, since they both rely on the goodwill of people to support them, would undoubtedly regard training of this kind as cynical and patently political in nature. But a realism about human nature is exactly what is required to survive and succeed as a nonprofit CEO.

Nonprofit literature, often the foundation of trainings which later accompany it, has tended to be as prosaic and blandly benevolent as the trainings and seminars and speeches it spawns. Nonprofit books invariably have been about prominent components of nonprofit institutions—effective boards, effective executives, effective fundraising: anything and everything but the political dimensions of these institutions. Nonprofit books have been about succeeding, about what makes a good executive good, or a great organization great, not about surviving. Apparently those who write about nonprofits do not think about the political dimensions of executive survival, or if they do think about it, they are perhaps reluctant to write about it because of its unseemly connection to conflict and failure, which are more the terrains of novelists than the success school of contemporary nonprofit literature. But as the nonprofit CEOs who have a professional history know, as the Doug Hays's of the profession know, one sometimes has to survive to succeed; and even when one is succeeding, survival may be waiting beyond the next horizon, waiting beyond the next capital campaign, the next budget, or the next presidential succession.

In my reading of nonprofit literature and my larger review of it for this book, I only encountered one book with the word survival in its title, **The Executive Director's Survival Guide: Thriving as a Nonprofit Leader**. Just looking at its title, I thought I had found the book that I wanted to write, but after reading it I realized it had almost nothing in it about executive survival. Instead it dealt deftly with topics like executive leadership, professional development, organizational effectiveness, managing change and sustaining a vision, fundraising, financial management, and establishing relationships with board and staff and other partners. Only once in the entire book and only briefly did the authors deal with anything that even hinted at the ideas of conflict and of survival, and that was to advise nonprofit CEOs, under the sub-heading "What do you do if there are problems between you and the Board Chair," to "proffer the olive branch to a difficult Board Chair" and to ask for a meeting to "clear the air." If the meeting failed to "reestablish the common ground" between the CEO and the Board Chair, then, the authors advised, wisely I think, that it would be "best for the Board Chair, as volunteer, to resign from the position and let someone who can work with the Executive Director step in." What I wanted to explore in **The Nonprofit Leader as Liberal Thinker** was what happens when the Board Chair refuses to resign. That question and others like it have a political dimension that nonprofit literature has left unexplored.

I cannot say that I have found the for-profit literature of the business world any more enlightening on the issue of executive survival, though I found a few writers eminently wise in other respects: Jim Collins on the idea of institutional greatness, Peter Drucker on the limits of a liberal education for the modern executive, and Henry Mintzberg on the true meaning of thinking strategically. But most of the business literature is largely unfulfilling professionally and intellectually. I cannot say that I am much interested in what comes from the gut of Jack Welch or from the business pedagogy of Noel Tichy, though both of them, to profoundly different degrees, share in the enormous success of the corporate colossus General Electric. What I have found in my own experience is that nonprofit executives who religiously read business books and little else lack the intellectual nourishment to generate new and innovative ideas, but even more than that, they tend to be narrow in their outlook, and they tend to lack both depth and breadth as professionals and as people. Business books, whether they are written for nonprofits or for-profits, all attempt to compartmentalize the professional life by removing it from the context of the whole life.

After reading the first epigraph of the first chapter of **The Executive Director's Survival Guide**, I was certain it would be a book to make a deeper connection between the professional life and the whole life. But the meaning of the epigraph, by Frances Hesselbein, which posited that tomorrow's leaders will not be focused on "how to do," but rather on "how to be," was left largely unfulfilled. **The Nonprofit Leader as Liberal Thinker**, by bringing a classical view of ethics to bear upon the often unsavory realities of professional life, will, I hope, fulfill the meaning of Hesselbein's wise observation, but the fundamental question of "how to be" will nevertheless be difficult to define. Defining how we should "be" will require reconciling two vastly different views of reality and of human nature: the cunning political pragmatism of Machiavelli with the virtuous philosophical idealism of Aristotle and of other thinkers from antiquity. For nonprofit CEOs, this discovery of "how to be" will require much more than their participation in professional training and much more moral and intellectual growth than reading business books can provide; it will require a lifelong education in the liberal arts so that the profession becomes part of a larger life lived well, so that information, of which the modern world has an abundance, becomes knowledge, and knowledge reflected upon, of which the modern world seems to have too little, becomes wisdom.

With all of my misgivings about nonprofit

training and nonprofit and for-profit literature, I wondered what kind of book could fill such a deep void in the life of a nonprofit CEO. What kind of book could propel these CEOs into the lifelong pursuit of wisdom that both integrates and transcends their profession? What kind of book could inspire them to be good not only at their profession, but at life itself? Would such a book need to tell a story, a story as much about surviving as succeeding? Would it be fiction or memoir? Would it be a non-fiction book imparting the kind of business advice that non-fiction business books impart? Or would it be a series of essays on topics like "The Politics of Nonprofits" or "Can Nonprofit CEOs Live the Good Life?" After reflecting on all of these possibilities, I decided that **The Nonprofit Leader as Liberal Thinker** would be part memoir, part business book, part extended essay on the political dynamics of nonprofits, and part philosophical meditation on the connection between the professional life and the whole of life lived well. I decided it would be the story, my story, of a nonprofit CEO and his rise and fall and eventual restoration.

To the extent that the tale I have to tell is

part essay on the political dynamics of nonprofits and on the philosophical dimensions of what it means to live life well, I have tried to distill the wisdom of this book through quotations, both modern and classical, and through maxims of my own making. The inspiration for distilling the meaning of this book into epigrammatic form comes from reading the greatest of all writers of maxims, LaRochefoucauld, a 17th century Frenchman whose observations about human nature still have relevance today, as evidenced by this maxim, which could easily have been written about the modern-day leadership of any kind of institution: "People too much taken up with little things usually become incapable of big ones."

My intention for **The Nonprofit Leader as Liberal Thinker** is to take up with the big things, with what Alan Bloom called the permanent questions. For nonprofit CEOs the most fundamental questions have to do with who they are as people and, within that larger context, who they are as professionals. What is their nature? What are their virtues? Or as we moderns might put it, what are their values Other fundamental questions have to do with their preparation. Should nonprofit leaders be educated as well as trained, and if so, what should they be educated to be? Other questions are political in nature. How does a nonprofit leader survive and prevail when the winds against him rise to gale force? Others are organizational in nature. What does it really mean for a leader to have vision? What does it mean to be able to think strategically? And what really makes a great organization great?

What I have set out to do is to rewrite Machiavelli's **The Prince** for the nonprofit CEO, but in looking back at antiquity as Machiavelli did I have tried to temper his legendary cunning with the nobility and compassion of a Marcus Aurelius, and I have tried to soften his dark worldview with the sunnier notion of the good life contained in the work of Plato and Aristotle.

But I begin with Machiavelli, who was wiser than anyone about beginnings.

1

Beginnings

Nonprofit CEOs can only survive
by reverting to their beginnings.

Is That Happening to You?

Foolishness befuddles leaders who,
having rushed in or not,
fail to take the measure of the field before them
and, therefore, fail to command it fully.

Momentous events in our professional lives are sometimes set in motion by the smallest act, in my case a telephone call I made to an old friend of mine, Jimmy McNally. We had gone to college together twenty years earlier, after which Jimmy went west to Seattle and I went east to New York, only to find that we had both circled back to the city where we first met. Jimmy McNally came back as the president and CEO of the United Way, and I as the executive director of another prominent nonprofit, the Youth Association International.

Jimmy's office was only a short walking distance from mine, but I suggested instead that he meet me on the top floor of a parking garage not far from our offices.

"And don't tell anybody where you're going," I said, "or who you're meeting with."

Jimmy, who had been an anti-war activist in our college days, laughed. "So you finally went FBI on me, huh Palermo?"

"Just be there in ten minutes."

The top floor of the parking garage was, as I had hoped, deserted. It was a dark, wintry day, exceedingly cold. The story I told Jimmy McNally that afternoon was of a nonprofit CEO in the midst of a palace coup.

"It started with staff complaining among themselves," I said. "They complained that their ideas were rejected without explanation. They complained that they were overworked and under-appreciated. Their feelings were hurt, their self-esteem diminished."

"Poor souls," Jimmy said, with a look of disdain to match the sardonic tone.

I was not unsympathetic. The self-esteem movement had invented a new entitlement: the right not to have one's feelings hurt. Clearly, my old friend Jimmy McNally was not a man of this post-Freudian therapeutic age.

"But instead of filing a grievance," I went on, "they went over the CEO's head and complained to board members whom they thought would be sympathetic to their cause."

Jimmy, his lips drawn down in a DeNiro-like look of contempt, shook his head dismissively.

"They found the sympathetic ear they were looking for," I said. "The chair of the human resources committee, who then convened two secret meetings with these staff members to gather incriminating evidence."

I paused, momentarily unable to continue.

Jimmy's arms sprang out from his sides, palms up in anticipation.

"This led to a report calling for the dismissal of the CEO, to be presented at the next board meeting."

The story now told, Jimmy McNally, a man whose deep-set eyes and perpetual look of disdain sometimes made his natural self assurance appear arrogant, looked at me in a deeply commiserative way, and said, "Is that happening to you?"

"No," I said. "It's happening to you."

Before the month was out, Jimmy McNally

made a quiet, dignified departure and within a matter of weeks was headed west again. I was not the only one to miss the fire and intensity Jimmy brought to our nonprofit community. Many of us missed the excitement, the energy, the intellect he brought to our town. I did not know it then, but years later I would suffer a similar fate, though the political storm that gathered around me would feel more like a hurricane than a thunderstorm, a hurricane that I might have avoided had I been wise enough to see it coming. And there was wisdom to be found in the circumstances surrounding the fall of Jimmy McNally, but I was not curious enough, nor was I unsettled enough, to see it. Things were simply going too well for me to consider the notion that a palace coup of this kind could be mounted against me. It just did not seem within the realm of possibility, given my growing stature in the community and the rising reputation of my agency. So, even though I missed my old friend and colleague, I never thought about the matter again, not until my own agency's palace coup was about to topple me. Then Jimmy McNally came east again to tell me what I should have known all along.

Obviously, what I told Jimmy McNally on that wintry day many years ago was not the whole story behind his departure. There was a political dimension to his circumstances that I had missed entirely. I knew there were some difficult personalities on his staff, most of whom he had handled less than adroitly, but I did not know how divided the board had been about hiring Jimmy. That division occurred when the chair of the human resources committee—the same person who had secretly and unprofessionally sought grievances from Jimmy's staff—had championed another candidate for the CEO position. The vote of the board that originally hired Jimmy had been a divided one, and when this powerful and influential chair of the human resources committee seized the opportunity to reverse it, those board members who had originally voted to hire Jimmy and who supported him when they thought things were going well, were now unwilling to take up the fight. I would one day miss the fault lines in my own agency, most of which were present before I ever came to town.

I almost did not come to town. I had spent the last decade working in Manhattan at the international headquarters of Youth Association International, the agency to which I had devoted my entire career, just recently going back to a local affiliate in a small city in upstate New York. We had been there about a year—my wife and I and our two daughters—when I got a call on a Friday night from the local affiliate in my hometown. I had worked for them for a few years after graduating from college, and then had gone to work for the international organization in New York. The caller was Danny Ackerman, whom I had known for many years and who had been on the board of directors when I previously worked for the organization. He was the chairman of the personnel committee.

Danny, a union steward with no tolerance for small talk, came quickly to the point: "We had to let our CEO go, and we decided we wanted to call you first before we opened the job up. Would you have any interest in coming back?"

"I don't think so, Danny, but thanks for thinking of me."

"You sure?"

"Well, we've only been here a year. I like my job, we really like the community. So I have to say no, but I'm flattered that you thought of me."

"Okay," he said. "If you change your mind, give me a call."

The next Friday I got a call from another member of the board asking me to reconsider, and I told him, as tactfully as I could, that my no was firm and final. The Friday after that, it was the director of planning for the city, a man who had been a longtime friend of my family. I got a call from an officer of the board the following week, and then Danny Ackerman again on that final Friday when I relented and agreed to meet with them.

"But just to talk," I said. "Not an interview."

"Fine, we'll just talk."

"Okay," I said, thinking that it would not hurt to extend them this courtesy, and it would give me an opportunity to visit my mother. "We'll talk."

By Monday Danny had already gotten back to me with the date, time and place of the meeting, which was to be with two members of the board, Greg Robertson and Peter Matthews, who were respectively the vice president of the board and the chairman of the nominating committee. That was all I knew about Robertson and Matthews. I would later learn that, although they held leadership positions on the board, they only represented one powerful faction on the board.

When I arrived at the restaurant where we were to meet, the place was deserted, so I went up to a waiter and explained my situation.

"No, you're in the right place," he said, pointing to two large double doors at the other end of the dining room. "They're in there."

I walked through those doors, expecting to find messers Robertson and Matthews. Instead I found a full buffet table and the entire board of directors. All I could do at this point was be as genial as I could, introducing myself to the board members I did not know, and renewing my acquaintance with those members I had known from my work with the organization more than a decade ago. It was a big board, forty members, and there had to be at least thirty of them there. At lunch I ended up sitting with some members I knew and a few I had met for the first time, and quickly took note of the fact that neither Robertson nor Matthews was at my table.

As lunch ended, chairs started to be repositioned until they formed a semi-circle around me, the heir apparent. As soon as the scrape and bustle of this movement subsided, Danny Ackerman, the gentleman who had originally called me, asked me a rather open-ended interview question, to which I replied as politely as I could that I had not come to town to apply for their CEO position. I had come to talk only, to have a conversation about the agencies circumstances and its future. So talk it was, interspersed with a few more interview-like questions, which I dutifully dodged, until the larger meeting concluded and the real meeting commenced, the one with messers Robertson and Matthews.

Greg Robertson, the first vice president of the board, was exactly a year away from assuming the presidency. In his early fifties, he was a tall, graying and decidedly handsome man who had made a small fortune in the insurance business. His counterpart, Peter Matthews, was on the other side of fifty, taller, leaner, more intense. He was not an officer of the board, but had a position that was even more influential: chairman of the nominating committee. Whereas Greg Robertson conveyed the affability of a salesman, Peter Matthews, the third generation owner of a successful industrial supply company, was the quintessential bottom line businessman: as pointed in his personality as he was in his appearance.

In the presence of Peter Matthews, even a talker like Greg Robertson listened. As did I. "Okay," Peter Matthews said, his sharp facial features seemingly cutting through me as well as to the chase. "We've had our talk." He seemed to come down on the word "talk" with enough sarcasm to be playful but not demonstrably unpleasant. "Now here's our offer." Which was quite generous: the salary alone was considerably more than what they paid their previous CEO. "We'll give you the weekend to consider it," he said. "We'd like an answer by Monday."

Monday's deadline came and went. I had left the Friday meeting with Matthews and Robertson thinking that as a courtesy I would wait until Monday to tell them what I had already known: that I did not want the job, however good their offer. But by Monday my wife and I had begun to consider it, and by the end of the week the reasons for taking the job not only seemed more persuasive, the thought of returning to our hometown suddenly appealed to us.

So a few weeks later, after I had negotiated what I thought was a very good contract, we headed west, this time to our hometown and to a professional homecoming for me that was fraught with difficulties I had not—but should have—anticipated. The forewarnings were there from the beginning, but I had not looked and, therefore, had not seen what was coming.

Machiavelli, who is almost without peer—the one exception being Aristotle—as a political thinker in the west, gave wise counsel in his **Discourses on Livy** on the importance of beginnings. Although Machiavelli was not writing about individual leaders when he wrote that "states can only survive by periodic reversions to their beginnings," his insight applies to nonprofit CEOs, who can only survive by reverting to their beginnings, to their entry into the institutions they are hired to lead. They can only survive by marking that moment in time as a way of understanding the true nature of the institution, its traditions, its aspirations, its divides. Otherwise foolishness befuddles leaders who, having rushed in or not, fail to take the measure of the field before them and, therefore, fail to command it fully. I would learn how to command the field before me from one of the most charming Machiavellians I have ever met. He was the president of the board, though he was not at my "interview" luncheon. He had not been one of the board's representatives who called me originally, nor had he played any role in the negotiation of my contract. But on my first day on the job, waiting for me, seated regally on the sofa in my office, was the man himself, Tommy DiTullio.

The Politician President

It has never been politic for me
to let another know my heart.
~John Williams, Augustus

Tommy DiTullio was the twelfth of thirteen children of Italian immigrant parents.

"I'm Calabrese," he said shortly after introducing himself on that first day in my office.

He had leaned forward to shake my hand, then sat back with an air unlike the southern Italian he had just revealed himself to be, and more like a Florentine nobleman, his white shirt standing out in contrast to his olive skin and silver-gray hair. "And you?" he said.

"Sicilian."

"Sure," he said, "the city of Palermo, and the map of Sicily on your face."

"So," I said, making an effort to be cordial, "I'm not sure if the map of Sicily on one's face is a compliment or a criticism?"

"A compliment. Sicily is one of the most beautiful places in the world. Italians have great respect for the Sicilians. Somebody, I don't remember who, said that anything an Italian can do, a Sicilian can do better."

"Luigi Barzini," I said.

Tommy DiTullio nodded, impressed.

"In a book called **The Italians**," I added.

The thought occurred to me that I had made a monumental mistake, that the board had somehow conspired to keep Tommy DiTullio away from me until I got here. He had in one moment suggested that my face had the hilly topography of Sicily and in the next engaged in shameless flattery with the Barzini reference to Sicilian superiority.

"This book," Tommy said, "it's about Sicilians?"

"One chapter is."

"You like to read, huh? You like a good story?"

"Both," I said, giving Tommy DiTullio the opening he needed to begin regaling me with stories of growing up in the Little Italy section of town and of working as the mayor's assistant in a career spanning almost forty years.

"I lived on macaroni and chicken soup," he said, "and anything I could steal from the fruit stands on Liberty Street. Today you got all these WASPS eating pasta. What the hell is pasta? It's macaroni or spaghetti. That's what we called it when I was a kid."

Tommy DiTullio was a survivor. He saw three mayors come and go. The fourth and current mayor fired him on her first day in office.

"I wasn't for her," he said, "but I tried to make her think I was. I made the mistake of letting some people close to me know what I really thought of her. There are times when you don't let anybody know what you really think. When you play the Irishmen's game with them. When you talk in riddles. But no one—not even the mayor—could say that the city paid out even one major claim during my tenure. A claim back then was either an act of God or it went away after I personally delivered a gallon of homemade wine to the injured party."

Although we had not talked at all about the organization, other than Tommy mentioning that he was the current board president with one year remaining of his two- year term, it was clear to me that my education in the art of politics had begun. And if I was initially unappreciative of his showing up unannounced, I found him engaging and would have preferred to continue our conversation. But it was my first day and there were other things that required my attention, so I stood up to signal that it was time for Tommy to leave.

I pulled my appointment book out of my suit jacket pocket and opened it. "Why don't we schedule some time to get together," I said.

"To do what?" Tommy said as he stood up and poured what remained of his coffee into the base of a plant next to the sofa. "The coffee is good for the plant," he said.

"To get better acquainted," I said, "to talk about the organization, where we're headed…"

Tommy slipped into a cloth coat that he would later try to pass off as cashmere, and waved a hand at me dismissively. "We can talk any time," he said. "We don't need to make an appointment. That's what you do with a WASP like Matthews: you make appointments." Tommy laughed at this and headed for the door.

I was, like Tommy DiTullio's WASPS, bound by time, by appointments, by administrative routine. "So when will I see you again?"

"Tomorrow," I could barely hear him say.

"When tomorrow?"

But Tommy DiTullio, the politician president, the man who would one day play the Irishman's game with me and I with him, who would one day keep his own Delphic counsel concerning me as I would with him, was gone.

Divided Loyalties

Who do you work for?
I work for you.

The rest of my first day was equally enlightening. I met with several key staff members, the most notable of whom was actually my predecessor, Matt Mihalak. I was originally told that the board had terminated Matt's employment, but in actuality they had only demoted him.

"To what position?" I asked him.

"I don't know," he said as the paper he held in his hand rattled from the nervous trembling of his hand.

"So no one told you what your job was?"

"I think everyone assumed you would determine that, which is why I brought my resume for you to look at."

Matt Mihalak pushed the now half-mangled resume across the conference table to me. "As my resume indicates," he said, "I have a really strong program background, and I could really be a big asset to you. I'm a hard worker. And if anything, I'm loyal. As anyone who knows me will tell you, loyalty has always been at the top of my list of priorities."

While Matt Mihalak waxed philosophically about the importance of loyalty, I quickly read his resume.

"Very impressive," I said. "With your strong program background, you shouldn't have any trouble finding what you're looking for."

"But I'm not looking to go anywhere," he said as if I had misunderstood him.

But I understood him perfectly, loyalty oath and all, and what I clearly wanted him to do was to go anywhere but here.

Doris Slater, a tough-talking woman with an unadorned look about her, followed Matt Mihalak into my office. She was even more direct about where her loyalties lay. "I think Matt got railroaded. You may not have had anything to do with it, but as far as I'm concerned you have no business being here. That's the way I feel, and I'm not going to apologize for it."

Howard Sinden was next. Howard was old guard. He had been with the organization for thirty years, having befriended me when I went to work for the organization years ago after graduating from college. A fine gymnast in his youth, he still looked fit enough to do a routine on the parallel bars. He was pleased to see me and held onto my hand an extra moment after giving it a vigorous handshake.

"So, how did it go with those two?" Howard said.

Howard had stayed in touch with me over the years, and I trusted him. "Not particularly well. But why do you say 'those two'?"

Shoulders shrugged; eyes rolled.

"Isn't Mihalak married?"

"To a wallflower."

"Slater is no wallflower," I said.

"No," Howard said as he looked around the room with an amused look on his face, "she's anything but that."

"What is it?" I said, inspecting his inspection of my office.

"They obviously cleaned this place up before you got here," Howard said. "There were folding tables set up all around the room, with papers piled halfway up the walls. This office, the whole damn place for that matter, complete chaos."

"So is everybody lined up into two camps?" I said. "Or will I find more as I go?"

"There are two," Howard said, "mine and Mihalak's."

"And the board?"

"Two that I know of."

The only other staff member I encountered that day was my bookkeeper/secretary, who wanted me to know that she had a good working relationship with the board. My only advice to her, and I was quite clear on this point, was: "Just remember one thing. You work for me, not the board."

I apparently was not clear enough. She quickly called a board member about a decision I made, then told me, as she quoted this higher authority, "We really can't do it that way."

"No," I said. "What we can't do is break rule number one. What is rule number one?"

"I don't know what you mean?" she said.

"Who do you work for?"

She hesitated; looked away. "I work for you," she said, finally.

"That's right," I said. "So I trust this will never happen again."

And for her, it never did. She tossed her keys onto my desk at the end of the day and walked out of the office and never came back. I would not be so lucky with the others.

Friends and Enemies

We have no permanent allies, only permanent interests.
~Palmerston

I quickly learned this about Tommy DiTullio, who was back in my office the next morning, coffee in hand: If Will Rogers never met a man he did not like, Tommy DiTullio never met a man he did not know, for that morning Tommy told me we were going out to make the rounds. My office was in the center of what everybody called Downtown, a business district of banks, law firms, government offices. The retail trade had long since moved to suburban malls. There were not many people on the street at mid morning, but everyone who was there knew Tommy DiTullio. And when there was no one on our side of the block, Tommy had us cross over so we could engage every living soul on the street that morning.

"Ciotti," Tommy called out to a young, dark-haired, bowling ball of a man who did not notice us at first even though we had crossed the street to encounter him.

"Tommy DiTullio," Tommy said, extending his hand to the young man.

"Oh, yes," Ciotti said. "Mr. DiTullio. You're the mayor's assistant, right?"

"Used to be, kid. I'm retired."

Tommy then inquired about David Ciotti's mother, father, his aunt and uncle, two of his cousins and his parish priest. Tommy seemed to know more about David Ciotti's family than David Ciotti did. After telling the kid—to Tommy, apparently, everybody was a kid—a story about Ciotti's great uncle, who had grown up with Tommy in the Little Italy section of town during the Great Depression, Tommy introduced me: "I want you to meet the new director of the Youth Association, Michael Palermo."

"The Youth Association," Ciotti said. "I interviewed for a job there once."

"And you didn't get it?" Tommy said. "A

nice guy like you."

"I had two interviews. The one with the board member went okay, the one with the director did not."

"The one with Mihalak," Tommy said.

"Yeah, that's the guy."

"So that interview did not go very well, huh?" Tommy said.

Ciotti's face flinched.

Tommy would not let it go. "C'mon, David, you can tell me. I'm the president of the board of directors."

"I'm not going to get anybody in trouble, am I?"

Tommy waved off the kids' concern. "Nobody's gonna get in trouble. You can tell me, kid, I'm practically your uncle."

Amazingly, Tommy had gone from stranger on the street to Uncle Tommy in a matter of minutes.

The kid caved. "Well, okay," he said. Tentatively at first, then with the agitation of one who felt aggrieved, he described an office piled with paper and an interviewer, Mihalak, who paced the floor like a caged animal. The coup de grace came when Mihalak lunged at him with a pen poised as a knife, and shouted, "What would you do if a kid came up to you with a knife?"

"I was stunned," Ciotti said. "I didn't know what to say."

"Uh huh," Tommy said, cueing the kid to continue.

"So I told him I'd call the police, and he shouted, wrong answer, you never call the police. And that was the end of the interview."

Tommy patted David Ciotti on the shoulder. He told David to be sure to give his mom and dad Tommy's best.

Then we were off to the next encounter. We turned onto State Street, the city's main street that divided it east and west, and passed City Hall where Tommy had spent virtually all of his adult life deftly handling claims against the city. As we passed the front entrance of city hall, a building dominated by bright brick and smoked glass, the mayor's top assistant and two aides were walking to a waiting car. Tommy greeted them warmly, respectfully. It was a greeting one might characterize as perfectly proportioned—the perfect mean between distaste and devotion.

"Those guys friends of yours?' I asked him as we headed up State.

Tommy rolled his eyes.

"Could have fooled me," I said.

"You can never let your enemies know what you're thinking," Tommy said, "because they might be your enemy one day and your friend the next. Or your friend might be your friend one day and your enemy the next. It all depends on what is important to you at the time. My interest with them is in seeing to it that the Youth Association continues to get a good grant from the city every year."

"You just took a page from Palmerston," I said

"Who?"

"A British Prime Minister."

"Really?" Tommy said in a buoyant, self-satisfied tone.

"You must have learned that at Oxford or at the Kennedy School at Harvard."

"Don't laugh," Tommy said. "You remember Mayor Mariella. I worked for him for 20 years. I heard they studied him at Harvard. Me? Ward politics was my college. I got my Ph.D. in it. So maybe you should start calling me doctor."

"Okay, Doctor."

"And if I was a doctor, my field would be

Roman history, the Roman Empire."

"What about the Greeks?"

"The only thing I like about the Greeks is their hot dogs."

And that, I came to realize, was vintage Tommy DiTullio. He could operate with the high and the low, with the cultivated and the coarse, but fundamentally he was the twelfth of thirteen children of Italian immigrant parents who was streetwise enough to carve out a storied career in local politics. This was a man, or as Tommy himself would say, a guy, on whom nothing was lost, and from whom I could learn many things.

As we continued up State Street, I kept going back to the encounter with David Ciotti. '"Tommy, is that one of the reasons Mihalak got fired, the Ciotti incident?"

"No, that's the first time I heard it. And we never really fired Mihalak. Well, we did; then we took it back. I wanted to fire him, but the WASPS wanted to keep him on because they said he was too good a program guy to let go. So we demoted him."

"And now he's my problem," I said.

"Yes, and you know that old adage, that you keep your friends close and your enemies closer?

That doesn't apply here. This Mihalak kid has too much pride. If you let him hang around, he will bring you down. He will do it out of envy and ambition."

"My Iago," I said.

"Who?"

"Iago. Othello."

"Never heard of those guys. Are they from Oxford?"

"Sort of," I said. "They're characters in Shakespeare."

Tommy shook his head. The expression on his face was more amused than perplexed. "You got me puzzled," he said. "But what you find in a book, I can find on the street. But wherever you find it, it takes a little thinking to figure it out."

"You've obviously thought about this Mihalak situation."

"Yes, and he needs to go before The Ides of March," Tommy said.

"You do know Shakespeare."

"I was supposed to read it in high school, but I never really read it."

"So if I don't get rid of this guy, he and his friends are going to stab me to death, figuratively speaking."

"Probably. But you have to remember that Mihalak has a stinger in Greg Robertson, who will be president a year from now."

"A stinger?"

"Yeah, you know. Mihalak's his boy. Robertson thinks Mihalak is the greatest when it comes to programming for the kids."

"So what are you telling me, Tommy?"

"I'm telling you it won't be easy. You make a move on Mihalak and you'll be breaking a rule you should try never to break."

"What rule is that?"

"Always respect a dog for its master."

By this time we had circled back to my office, in front of which Tommy's compact car was parked. The car, as nondescript as its owner was flamboyant, was more suited to a machine politician than an Italian prince. "One more stop," he said as we settled into Tommy's car. "I want you to meet this guy. I think he would be good for us."

"How so?"

"This guy is going to be running this town some day. He wants to make his mark in politics."

Tommy was right. Bobby Hathaway was a baby-faced lawyer just a few years out of law school who was about to become a partner in a major law firm and the campaign manager of the city's next mayor. Although Tommy was an FDR Democrat and an admirer of JFK, he apparently had no reservations about walking into the lobby of Bobby's law firm, which was noted for its support of Republican politicians, and insisting he see Attorney Hathaway without an appointment. When we walked into the lobby, I was carrying a cardboard file box that Tommy had given me containing a gallon of homemade red wine and a prosciutto the size of a small tree trunk. Tommy gratuitously told the law firm's receptionist that the file box contained papers in a very important case being handled by Attorney Hathaway. The receptionist certainly could have drawn that conclusion herself. But Tommy had a flair for fibbing, in which he unabashedly reveled. And when necessary, he had an even greater flair for lying. The fibbing was nothing more than playful mischief. The lying, I would learn, was part of a jaded political personality that compelled him, as one of my Chicago friends, John Markley, would have described it, to "grease the skids" when he could and "do unto others before they do it unto you" when he could not.

As for Bobby Hathaway, the boy wonder

with the cherubic smile, he was unavailable to meet with us that day, but Tommy met with him soon after that, and Bobby accepted his invitation to serve on the Board of Directors of the Youth Association.

When Tommy reported this back to me, I said, "You made this guy's election to the board sound like a fait d'accompli."

"What, you don't want the guy?"

"I didn't say that."

"What, we gotta convene a committee to bring a guy onto the board?"

"You could have told me what you wanted to do," I said.

"Okay, next time I'll ask. We'll dialogue," Tommy said, adding a note of ironic emphasis to the word dialogue. "How's that?"

Fine, I thought, and laughed even though its implication that he was reconstituting the board almost entirely on his own would prove to be quite the opposite of fine. He had done this reconstituting under the innocent eye of my predecessor and would continue to do it under my own accommodating eye.

"Yeah," I said, still laughing. "We'll dialogue."

The Power of Appointment

CEOs who want to control their own destinies
must be willing to wield power,
particularly the power of appointment to the board

I did not know it then, but roughly half the forty member board of directors had developed a taste for Tommy DiTullio's homemade red, which he personally delivered to their homes on holidays, and most of them would follow Tommy's lead when it became apparent that his interests no longer matched mine. Palmerston proved to be correct: my friend Tommy, my uncle Tommy—for over time he did become like an uncle to me—would become my enemy.

How Tommy managed to bring so many people onto the board during Peter Matthews's tenure as nominating chairman was not as perplexing as it looked. Peter was running a business, Tommy was retired, and each of them had a different reference point to power. Tommy concentrated on the average board member, of whom there was a larger number. These were men and women of modest means and limited influence whom Tommy could empower by galvanizing them into a group. Peter Matthews was content to concentrate on the leadership of the board, handpicking the president-elect, Greg Robertson; the first vice-president, Diandra Gray, the wife of a prominent surgeon; and the second vice-president, Chuck Lauer, the president and CEO of his own computer applications company. Peter Matthews's philosophy was based on what he called the golden rule: those who had the gold, ruled. He was completely oblivious, as was I at first, to the power of prosciutto and red wine.

One afternoon just after a board meeting concluded, Peter Matthews took me aside and said, "I hear Tommy is spending an awful lot of time here."

"Who said that?" My hunch was Mihalak.

"It doesn't matter who told me."

Tommy was standing nearby, talking to two other board members.

"Yeah, he comes around once in a while," I said.

"I hear it's just about every day."

I wondered how often Peter talked to Mihalik. I was tempted to say something to him about staff going over my head to board members, but decided not to.

"That's not a healthy situation, Michael. The other board members are going to resent it. They're going to feel left out of the loop. You need to talk to him."

"I'll see what I can do," I said.

"Because if you don't," Peter said, "I have to reconsider whether I'm going to stay on this board."

"I'll see what I can do, Peter."

"Fine," he said, and as he walked away, Tommy turned from the two board members he was talking to and said to Peter: "I liked your comments on the financial statement today, Matthews."

Peter always asked a question or two about the financial statement, even if it was just to hear himself talk.

"Matthews, you're a good man, Matthews," Tommy added.

Peter barely nodded Tommy's way as he walked out of the building. For all Tommy's talk about not letting people know what you really think, he had just revealed to Peter Matthews that he was willing to be impertinent to him in public. This was the same Tommy DiTullio who admonished me about the hazards of human pride.

After everyone else had gone, Tommy and I sat down in the boardroom and talked.

"Peter thinks you're spending too much time here," I said. "He thinks other members of the board are starting to resent it."

"Tell him to come down more often," Tommy said. "Tell him we can dialogue."

"Just what I need," I said.

"Don't worry about Matthews," Tommy said. "I'll take care of Matthews."

And that is how we left it that day, with Tommy's promise to handle a problem he had largely created himself—a board divided along lines of personal loyalty: Tommy's old guard and young turks against the succession of leaders Peter Matthews had lined up. If I did nothing about the time Tommy spent with me, I would alienate the board leadership that was about to succeed him. If I distanced myself from Tommy, I would alienate a board president with a year left on his term. Taking sides was inevitable, but I did it by default, by drift, by indecision. I did not aggressively take a position, nor did I look closely at where the other volunteers were positioned in the bifurcation of the board. There were a few members of the old guard who were actually loyal to the leadership that Peter Matthews had formed, and when the influence of Peter's leadership group began to wane—all but one of them would eventually resign—this particular old guard group held me responsible for the departure of the leadership group, and eventually supported Tommy in the palace coup that coalesced against me.

Deferring to Tommy DiTullio the task of handling Peter Matthews's increasing disaffection was an error in judgment on my part, and it was symptomatic of a larger problem of deferring to Tommy on many matters, the most notable being the recruitment and retention of board volunteers. CEOs who want to control their own destinies must be willing to wield power, particularly the power of appointment to the board. Nonprofit CEOs cannot survive, nor can they succeed, without taking control of the board nominating process. Not only did I not control that process; I had ceded its control to one socially adept, politically astute person, Tommy DiTullio, and a board of directors recruited and retained by the efforts of one person or one committee chair is a board poised to bring down a CEO at the slightest provocation. All I had to do was offend Tommy or alienate one of his friends on the board and that would be provocation enough for a large contingent of the board to line up against me. Mihalak, after all, was demoted for reasons that seemed to have almost nothing to do with performance and just about everything to do with conflicts of personality.

If I made a major error in judgment by ceding control of the board nominating process to Tommy DiTullio, I could have overcome the error by being more careful and more diligent in determining where every board member stood in the organization, where their loyalties lay, and to whom each was connected by commerce, by friendship, by common interest. If I had taken Machiavelli's advice about the importance of beginnings, I would have discovered the connection between some of the old guard group and Peter Matthews's leadership group, and by doing so I easily could have persuaded Tommy to let the terms of the old guard group expire at a time when their interests were contravene to Tommy's. This would have been possible in the early days of my tenure because Tommy viewed anyone favorable to a WASP like Peter as a potential adversary. Once Peter Matthews and his leadership group were gone, I should have moved to phase out their friends and supporters on the board. It was an opportunity that I missed and one I would sorely regret.

If my attention to the recruitment and retention of the board suffered from benign neglect, my concentration on the composition of the staff did not. Although I had the immediate problem of replacing my secretary/bookkeeper who resigned after my first day on the job, I decided to replace her with someone from a temporary agency until my staff reorganization was ready for presentation to the personnel committee. I needed board approval of the plan because I was proposing the creation of new positions, particularly a director of operations, the phasing out of other positions, and the establishment of a policy that would give me the authority to hire and fire.

I was confident, as was Tommy, that the board would support the plan, but neither of us was confident the personnel committee would support it.

"The only votes you can count on from the

committee," Tommy said, "are me and Danny Ackerman. Then you got the WASPS who will want you to make Mihalak your director of operations."

"I take it you didn't appoint those people to the personnel committee?"

"I didn't appoint anybody," Tommy said.

"As the board president, you have the power to appoint anybody to any committee you want."

"So I have that power, huh?" Tommy said as he looked past me and out my office windows to the street below and the city beyond, the pensive politician in him, thinking, calculating, strategizing. "Then I'll appoint a new personnel committee," he said finally, his eyes—enormous, caramel-colored eyes made even larger by their bug-like protuberance—coming back to meet mine.

"I don't think your friends from Fairview would appreciate that, Tommy." Fairview was the affluent suburb where many of Tommy's WASPS lived. "Wouldn't it be wiser to reorganize all the committees? That's something you could have done, and probably should have done, at the beginning of your term as president."

Tommy, his already prominent chin tightened in mock distaste and his high forehead furrowed in pleasant surprise, had the look of a man pleased with his political protégé. "Michael," he said, "you're learning. You still need training, but you're definitely learning."

Tommy was equally pleased with the tactics to follow. I drafted a cover memo from Tommy and a committee survey which we sent out to all of the members of the board asking them to indicate on which committee or committees they preferred to serve. The survey asked for a first, second and third choice, and had as its disclaimer that every effort would be made to appoint them to a committee of their choice (not **the** committee of their choice), while also taking the overall needs of the organization into consideration.

It soon became apparent to me that Tommy, like Shakespeare, whom he had not read, and Machiavelli, whom he intuitively imitated but did not know, was a monarchist, and he relished the idea of determining the committee assignments of his colleagues on the board. He did not seem to care which particular committee anyone served on, only that he had the power to determine it. And though he did take some pleasure in appointing a few of his colleagues to the building committee—a committee that rarely met, and one that Tommy regarded as the equivalent of political oblivion—he left it to me to decide who would serve on what committee. For the most part I followed the survey preferences of individual board members, but in a few instances I did not. My strategy, which turned out not to be a strategy at all but a short-term tactic, was to get the personnel committee reconstituted so I would have sufficient support for my reorganization and for the policy authority to hire and fire. If I had been thinking strategically I would have given greater consideration to the overall committee structure and to the composition of the nominating committee, which is the real fulcrum of power in a nonprofit institution. But at the time I was content to defer to Tommy DiTullio, who had become a one-man nominating committee and a power unto himself.

Clarifying the Lines of Authority

The clarification must be as much about what they are not asked to do, as what they are asked to do.

Hiring a director of operations was the centerpiece of my reorganization plan, but what

I was really doing was hiring a hatchet man to do the dirty work I preferred not do myself. I could not do it partly because I realized that those who wield the ax must ultimately succumb to it, but mostly because I did not have the temperament for it. I also realized that most of the key staff whom I believed would be better off elsewhere were connected to one board member or another. Just as the leadership group supported Matt Mihalak, there were old guard members who thought a long-term employee like Howard Sinden should be left untouched by any reorganization. Howard was only three years away from retirement, and there was sentiment on the board that he ought to be allowed to finish his career in a dignified manner. The leadership group wanted Matt Mihalak kept on because he was, as the second vice president Chuck Lauer observed, "magical when it comes to programming." I was more sympathetic to Howard Sinden's situation. He had spent thirty years in the organization, and he deserved some consideration as his career neared its end, whereas Mihalak was a fallen leader with supporters still in power.

But the larger question regarding the staff was why so many of them were connected to members of the board, why so many of them had what Tommy liked to call a "stinger." The mistake Mihalak and his predecessor made was to agree to a policy which gave the board the power to hire and fire staff. This encroachment on the authority of the CEO was critical because it meant that personnel committee members not only approved job descriptions and salary ranges, all within reasonable scope of their authority, but also interviewed job candidates and hired and fired staff. The board, through the personnel committee, had attenuated the CEO's role as the undisputed leader of the staff. I needed to regain the authority to manage the staff while redefining the lines of authority between board and staff. If I could not ultimately stop the Mihalaks of the world from going over my head to board volunteers, I could make their professional life more challenging by ratcheting up the supervision and scrutiny of their work. I could make them think seriously about the advisability of moving on. But I could not make these staff changes myself. I needed someone else to wield the ax. I needed a director of operations.

Part of the way through the interview process for the director of operations position, I got a call from Danny Ackerman. I had kept Danny on the personnel committee, but not as chairman. I had instead chosen Brian Billingsley, a young labor attorney who supported the reorganization and the changes in policy.

"Michael, I hear you're interviewing for the director of operations job."

"I'm about halfway through," I said.

"Is Billingsley involved?"

"No, nobody from the board is involved," I said.

"I just thought that Billingsley, as chairman of the personnel committee, labor lawyer…"

"Your suggestion is appreciated, Danny, and I know it comes with the best of intentions," I said, happy to have the opportunity to make this distinction, "but it has the unintended effect of undermining my ability to manage the organization. However much experience Brian has in this area, and he has a considerable amount, involving him in the interview process blurs the line of authority between me the management, and you the board."

"I understand," Danny said. "These are decisions that you and you alone have to make. I'm just trying to help out."

I liked the you-and-you-alone line. It indicated that I was making progress in more clearly delineating the responsibilities of board and management. "That's just not the help I need, Danny. I need you and your colleagues on the board to set policy, to set the strategic direction of the organization, approve my budgets, monitor finances and program outcomes. I need you to give money and raise money, lots of money. What I don't need is for you to try to manage the organization by interviewing prospective staff members. That's just not an appropriate role for the board."

Danny Ackerman accepted my explanation without any further comment. I had had my first Noel Tichy teachable moment, and I needed to have many more in the future if I was to educate the board properly as to the true nature of their responsibilities. One simply cannot expect that board volunteers will take away these understandings from an initial orientation, however good that orientation might be. Nor can one expect board volunteers to learn their proper role at conferences or through their experiences as volunteers in other organizations. All nonprofit CEOs must frequently don the professorial robe to clarify the lines of authority in the organization, and the clarification must be as much about what they are **not** asked to do as what they **are** asked to do. What board volunteers must always be asked to do can be distilled down to what Patrick McSweeney taught me long ago, and that is to have an impact on the organization, as donors, door-openers, doers and decision-makers—the four D's. Not that every board volunteer will perform all four. All of them should be donors who are willing to give and ask others to give. The remaining doing, door-opening and decision-making will vary depending on the volunteer's tenure, connections, and aspirations to lead. Hiring and firing, however, are two tasks that board members should be told **not** to do. CEOs who cannot hire and fire, who cannot command both of these processes from the first to the last, cannot manage, and therefore, cannot lead. I clearly had some leading to do in the hiring of a director of operations.

To Hire or not to Hire

Picking the right people is not a science but an art.

After wading through reams of resumes

and letters of introduction and after interviewing the three individuals whom I thought were the best candidates, I hired Evelyn Wagner to be my director of operations. Evelyn had a business degree, and she had been honorably discharged from the Army where she had gotten, among other things, supervisory experience. It was clear from my initial interview with her that she was not someone to be trifled with, which I thought was perfect for what she would be asked to do: bring order to a house that might otherwise collapse into chaos. What I liked about Evelyn Wagner was her toughness, her intelligence, and her organizational skills.

On her first day on the job Evelyn sensed my frustration with the temp I had retained to run the office and keep the books, and she made it her priority to find someone to fill the position permanently. In the next three weeks she screened dozens of candidates, interviewed several, and brought in to meet me the candidate she thought was the best, a stoical but highly skilled bookkeeper named Meg Michalski. I was impressed with Meg Michalski's office skills, particularly her business education and bookkeeping background, but I was unimpressed with and wary of a personality too Delphic to read.

"I don't think Meg is right for the job," I said to Evelyn after the interview. "I just don't have a good feel about it."

"But she has all the skills you're looking for. With her doing the books you sure as hell won't have to worry about going into a finance committee meeting with a sloppy and inaccurate financial statement."

I wondered if I had delegated too much authority to Evelyn. "I think I need to interview a few other candidates," I said.

"I personally don't think you need to, Michael. I think Meg Michalski is perfect for the position. Help me pinpoint what it is that you find problematic with her, and maybe we can work that out."

She's just too cool to read," I said. "I'm not sure that stoical persona is who she really is."

"I think it was just nervousness," Evelyn said. "I think she's more personable than what she showed today. Let me bring her back in for a second interview. If you still don't like her, then I'll bring in some other candidates for you to consider."

Meg Michalski was brought back in for a

second interview. She was more personable this time, smiling through much of the interview. Meg admitted to me much later—long after Evelyn Wagner had moved on—that Evelyn had prompted her to be more personable with me in the second interview. But at the time I naively believed that Meg Michalski had simply revealed a more open and affable aspect of her personality in the second interview. The real Meg Michalski was more like the person who showed up for the first interview. She was indeed stoical, and she did have a strong sense of duty to her work, about which she was, as Evelyn Wagner promised, highly skilled. But beneath the stoical exterior was a personality that was as discontented as it was dutiful, and it was this discontent that would ultimately be exploited by Tommy DiTullio and others in an attempt to topple me.

After reflecting on the situation surrounding Meg Michalski, I realized there were maxims that every CEO would be wise to contemplate. If it was unwise for a CEO to defer to the board in the arena of board development—in the cultivation, orientation, education, and retention of board volunteers—it was utterly careless to delegate the hiring of key staff, staff who report to the CEO, to an associate. It was not enough to be the final decision-maker in the hiring of key staff, because the final decision unduly reflected judgments made early in the hiring process. These early steps, from carefully reading resumes all the way to making appointment calls to candidates, were as important as the final step of making a decision.

In today's world, prospective employees are evaluated largely in terms of their skills, with the term "skill sets" becoming a cultural cliché. Prospective employees are not typically regarded as complex personalities who need to be properly read to be properly managed. They are instead a cobbled together collection of skills. Evelyn Wagner made much of the fact that Meg Michalsky was highly skilled, and Meg was indeed skilled as a bookkeeper and office manager. But the reality is that picking people largely on the basis of their skills is a form of executive foolishness. The reality is that any reasonably intelligent person can be taught the requisite skills of virtually any position a nonprofit might require, with the exception of highly educated health care professionals like doctors and psychiatrists. As

Machiavelli well understood, every leader must first be a shrewd judge of character. Picking the right people is not a science but an art. It is having the intuition to know who will be both loyal to you and to the mission of the organization. If I had followed my intuition with Meg Michalski and given greater attention to the task of hiring staff who report directly to the CEO, I would have saved myself and the organization considerable travail. But there would be more travail to go through first. For Evelyn Wagner had to finish the task of reorganizing the rest of the staff, of bringing order to the chaos, of moving the Mihalaks of the world to some other part of the nonprofit planet.

Overreaching

I knew that history and literature were full of examples of people who pushed things too far, who lacked a sense of moderation and proportion.

Although I lacked a strategic plan to work from (that would come later), I knew that the remainder of my reorganization required a programmatic plan. This in turn required the rudiments of a salary administration plan—

components like job descriptions and salary ranges—which I had already gotten approved by the personnel committee and by the full board. The overall strategy behind the reorganization was to put together a staff that was loyal to the institution, to its mission and vision (that would also come later), and to me personally as the leader of the institution (and that, for Mihalak and Slater and others, would never come at all). To facilitate the reorganization, I appealed to the tendency in Evelyn Wagner and in Matt Mihalak to overreach. I knew that history and literature were full of examples of people who pushed things too far, who lacked a sense of moderation and proportion, whether it was Achilles' defilement of Hector or the hubris of the modern-day jihadist. Evelyn Wagner, perhaps because of her military background, had a tendency to push the idea of order too far, and Matt Mihalak was full of the bravado of one who believed that his program skills were, as Chuck Lauer characterized them, magical. I knew I could use both of these tendencies—Evelyn's tendency to wind the organization's clock too tight, and Mihalak's to unravel and reinvent it—to create an organization in which loyalty and duty predominated. I did not have to do anything to get Evelyn to wield the ax; I simply had to stay out of her way. With Mihalak, all I had to do was let him reestablish and reinvent a program plan overreaching enough to take a magician to implement.

I took the new program plan to the board program committee. I did this because I wanted them to be aware of the ambitious benchmarks that the staff had established for the future of our program. It was also my first opportunity to clarify the board's limited role with respect to program. I wanted the board to understand that it had no real role to play in program development—though that is exactly what had been going on prior to my arrival—but it did have an important role in monitoring results. A few minutes into the meeting with the board program committee, I realized that the board committee reorganization that I had engineered had not gone far enough. The majority of the committee, which included the president-elect Greg Robertson and the second vice-president Chuck Lauer, were part of the Peter Matthews's leadership group, and as the meeting unfolded, two troubling themes emerged: the first was that a majority of them strongly disagreed with my decision to hire Evelyn Wagner instead of Matt Mihalak as the director of operations. Several committee members scoffed at virtually everything Evelyn said at the meeting and had nothing but high praise for Mihalak. This was not all bad: their hostility was directed almost entirely at Evelyn, the perfect buffer for me, and their enthusiasm for Mihalak blinded them to just how overreaching the program plan was. I knew that even if Mihalak was the magician many believed he was, he could not possibly pull off this plan in its entirety. But he could pull off part of it, which would have the effect of moving part of our program in a positive direction and moving Matt Mihalak in the direction of the door. The second theme that emerged came from Greg Robertson, who would be president in a matter of months, when he challenged the policy implications of the program plan. "I think our role goes beyond just monitoring results," he said, countering my argument for a more limited role for the board in program.

"Program development is not a proper role for the board," I said. "It's management's role; it's a staff function."

"What could be more proper than being

intimately involved in the program?" Robertson parried. "That's at the heart of what we do as a youth agency. It's at the heart of our mission as an organization."

"Our mission is at the heart of what we do as an organization," I said. "Not the program."

"But that's how we achieve our mission, isn't it?" Robertson said.

At this point I would have appreciated someone coming to my defense. I did not want to keep parrying with the future president of the organization, and I certainly did not want a difference of opinion with him to escalate to an adversarial level. I hoped that Evelyn might say something, but she had no real understanding of the proper role of board members in a nonprofit organization. And I was beginning to realize that Tommy DiTullio, who was ex officio on all committees by virtue of being president of the board, was not going to say anything either. Tommy rarely said anything at meetings. He would do all his talking and politicking and counting of votes before the meeting ever began. I had not done any politicking nor any vote counting, and with the way the program committee was constituted, I could not have done so even if I had wanted to.

"But how can you separate the two?" Robertson said. "We can't achieve our mission without program."

"I haven't separated them," I said. "What I've separated are the areas of responsibility. The board has the more important responsibility of the two—to protect the mission, and to make sure that everything we do, including program, is consistent with that mission. Management's job is to develop and implement the program, with the board monitoring results."

Chuck Lauer, a mountain of a man whose mind was as capacious as his body, took a different tack in coming to Greg Robertson's defense. "Keeping us out of program will eventually erode our support for it. People support that which they help to create," he said, adding the platitudinous to the political.

"Yes," I said, "and people support good things that others create, like the timeless mission that we've inherited from the founders of this great institution. Matt and Evelyn and I and the rest of the staff believe that this program plan rises to a level consistent with that historic mission."

Somehow the high-minded rhetoric and

the appeal to tradition worked, but not without the reminder of the link between the program and their magician Mihalak. The committee, after some additional grumbling, restrained their inclination to overreach and approved the plan, as did the full board, unanimously. I now had everything I needed—Evelyn's ax and Mihalak's magic—to clean the staff side of the house.

Levers of Power

The best board member to be nominating chair is one who is dedicated but disinterested.

The rest of my first year in the organization unfolded as I had hoped it would. Both Matt Mihalak and Doris Slater quickly ran afoul of Evelyn Wagner's reign of order. Mihalak simply could not comply with Evelyn's desire to know where he was and what he was doing every single minute of the day. Mihalak, despite his creative flair, had a tendency to get lost, whether it was shopping for supplies or going to some collaboration or inter-agency meeting that Evelyn regarded as a waste of time. With Evelyn and Doris it was just a matter of two immovable objects trying to move one another. And my decision to evaluate staff performance on a quarterly basis put additional pressure on everyone. When Slater's and Mihalak's first quarter evaluations did not go as well as they would have liked, I noticed that their effort, particularly Mihalak's, noticeably fell off. They started taking sick days, and before the year was out, Slater and Mihalak resigned. They both went to the same neighborhood community center, an agency that was expanding its youth programming and emerging as a serious competitor of ours. Mihalak and Slater not only left but took a key program with them, an outreach program that had been funded since its inception by city government. Matthews, Robertson and Lauer were in varying degrees irritated by these developments, publicly lamenting both the loss of Mihalak and of the more than $100,000 in funding for the program Mihalak took with him. During the board meeting at which these developments were announced, Peter Matthews drew another line, this one in stone rather than in sand. "If I were you," Matthews said, his pointed face pointed directly at me, "I'd go over to the city today and get that program back."

"I don't think that can be done," I said. "We as an organization don't have the relationship with the city. Matt Mihalak, on a more personal level, does."

"That may be. But what I'm telling you is, if we don't get it back, I don't see how I can stay on this board."

I did exactly as Peter Matthews advised and tried to get the program back. The person I had to persuade was David Sykes, the city's director of administration, a man who was as dry as he was able, a blunt-spoken bureaucrat with a flair for political in-fighting. But Sykes not only found my efforts unpersuasive; he apparently took some pleasure in thwarting them. It eventually got back to me and Tommy that Sykes said to one of his chief aides, "We're finally rid of the goombahs." Then a few years later Sykes hired Mihalak to work for the city, confirming for me what Peter Matthews publicly refused to accept: that the contract we had with the city had never been with our organization, but rather with Mihalak personally.

It was around this time when my belief about the value and efficacy of board committees had begun to diminish (hadn't someone once said that only two committees in history, the one that drafted the U.S. Constitution and the one that wrote the King James Bible, had ever accomplished anything worthwhile?) that I encouraged Tommy DiTullio to succeed Peter Mathews as the chair of the nominating committee. My reason for doing this was that Tommy was the only member of the board who took an active interest in recruiting new people for the board anyway, a fact which should have led me to just the opposite, paradoxical conclusion: that the best board member to be nominating chair is one who is dedicated but disinterested. With the annual meeting only weeks away, Tommy probably would have let the matter of the nominating chairmanship pass to the next administration if I had not brought it to his attention. But leaving the appointment to the discretion of Tommy's successor did not seem like a very good alternative either. My relationship with Greg Robertson was now strained—I hoped not irreversibly—by Mihalak's departure.

There was a third course I could have taken, one that, unfortunately, I never considered. I could have persuaded Tommy to appoint anyone I wanted to chair the nominating committee. I could have pushed for the appointment of one of the non-aligned members of the board who would perform their duties in a way that was disinterested and neutral rather than calculating and political, thus vesting most of the nominating powers in me, the CEO. There would come a time much later when Tommy would deeply resent my suggestion that someone succeed him as the nominating chair. Much later Tommy would come to understand that the nominating chair held the main lever of power in a nonprofit organization, and for me to suggest that he relinquish that lever would, as Palmerston promised, transform a trusted friend into a treacherous enemy. In the end, Tommy's interest was not in hope and opportunity for children but in power and influence for himself.

Lines of Communication

An unrestricted line of communication between staff and board is an invitation to trouble.

The war that was my reorganization had another casualty, Howard Sinden. It was the kind of casualty one could only characterize as collateral damage. It was certainly not my intention to drive Howard out of the organization: He had faithfully given more than thirty years of his life to the organization, almost all of it as a physical education director. Only recently had Mihalak appointed him to an administrative position. Mihalak had rightly recognized that Howard's interest in and passion for counseling kids and teaching sports like gymnastics had diminished over the years, and when Howard asked for an administrative position, Mihalak gave it to him. The problem was that Howard had been a fine physical education teacher and counselor, but was not as fine as an administrator.

Evelyn Wagner knew nothing about Howard Sinden's accomplishments as a counselor and coach. All she saw was an employee whose production was modest and whose workday was dominated by a desire to go home for dinner. But as soon as Mihalak and Slater left the organization, Evelyn turned her attention to Howard. He tried to accommodate her at first, but accommodations cannot be made with bureaucrats bent on control. When Howard complained to me, I tried to intercede on his behalf. I told Evelyn that I wanted her to lower the heat on Howard. But Evelyn's lowered heat was still hot enough to torment the pride and weaken the will of my old friend. Howard burst into my office unannounced one afternoon, and with an emotional intensity I had never seen Howard display—his breathing was so labored that he was hyperventilating—told me he was resigning. Reminded of the old Sicilian aphorism that anger clouds one's judgment, I said, "Howard, you're not in the right frame of mind to make a decision like that."

"How can you be in any other frame of mind with that…that..."

"I don't want you to resign, Howard."

"Then she'll have to go," he said.

"Can't you hang in there a little longer?" I said.

"No, I can't. I'm resigning now, before I have another heart attack."

"You had a heart attack?"

"Yes, and I'm not having another one because of that…"

"Then at least let me work out some kind of retirement package for you."

"Work out whatever you want," he said, and walked out of my office. I tried to work out a part-time, stay-at-home job for him doing some research and writing for our upcoming centennial celebration, but he declined. He did accept my offer to cover his health insurance until he was sixty-five. I never spoke to Howard after that. I only saw him once in the years since. I was walking up State Street one summer afternoon and Howard's car pulled up beside me. The windows of his car were closed so I could not hear what he said, but I could plainly see what he now thought of me with his middle finger brandished in anger and defiance. My old mentor, the man who taught me the art of changing a child's life, was now, and would forever remain, my bitter enemy.

Other staff members were driven out of the organization by Evelyn Wagner's iron hand. Most of them were young people with limited experience. I might have been able to inspire in them a sense of loyalty to me and to the vision I would ultimately forge for the organization, but because the purge and Evelyn's vigilant execution of it alienated virtually every faction on the board, I had more pressing problems to consider: what to do with Evelyn Wagner—board members were already demanding that something be done—and how to rebuild the staff. But both of these matters would have to wait for that transfer of power called the annual meeting.

A very troubled year had passed. Tommy DiTullio's term as president was coming to an end and Greg Robertson's was about to begin. It was a time for me as the CEO to reflect on the accomplishments of the year. Our by-laws required that I give a State of the Organization Address at the Annual Meeting, and there were, astonishingly—given everything that had gone on in the organization—positives to report: children served, results achieved, dollars raised. But as the day of the Annual Meeting approached, my reflections turned not to these positive outcomes but to the vicissitudes of my first year in the organization. I still had a house divided against itself. I still had a board with deep divisions, some of which I was still unaware. My staff reorganization had been a house-cleaning of such ferocity that it violated one of humanity's universal principles—a principle as true in the ancient world of Aristotle as it is in our modern world in which good is seemingly never absolute—the principle of moderation. Moderation is having a sense of proportion about all things. Moderation requires the wisdom not to push things so far that injustice becomes its true measure. I had allowed Evelyn Wagner to push things too far; I could not allow that to happen again. I would need to rebuild the structure that Evelyn and I had reduced to rubble, and I would need to do it in a way that was measured, moderate, fair. But the staff that I would rebuild would have to have a clearer understanding of the lines of authority in the organization. They would have to understand that their interaction with the board would be limited and circumscribed. They would have to realize that an unrestricted line of communication between staff and board is an invitation to trouble, to politicking, to disloyalty and division, and though labor lawyers routinely warn CEOs that they cannot terminate staff for going behind their backs to the board, CEOs must make the point, as many times as it is necessary, that going behind their backs is unqualifiedly unacceptable.

This does not mean that staff should be cut off from the board completely. There are times when staff interaction with the board is essential. Strategic planning, though primarily a board responsibility, invariably benefits from the unfettered observations of key staff members. Program committees cannot function properly without staff involvement. Board fundraising almost always requires staff support. But the

CEO must be the conduit through which board and staff communicate and collaborate. The CEO, in consultation with committee chairs, should convene and attend all committee meetings; and should be, per the organization's bylaws, an ex-officio member of all committees. This level of committee involvement is achievable if the number of standing committees is kept to a minimum—preferably no more than three—and greater use is made of tasks groups which only require a short-term commitment to manage.

When board and staff communicate outside the formal structure of committees or the exigencies of fundraising, very often trouble is imminent. I have often told board volunteers that, if a staff member brings a complaint directly to them, listen patiently, explain that the proper thing to do is to bring their concern to my attention, then immediately report it to the CEO. It is not the proper role of board to solve staff problems, unless their help is sought by the CEO. It is their proper role to report it, however—quickly, completely, accurately. The same holds true if the communication goes in the other direction: board complaining to staff. Staff members should respectfully listen, tell the board volunteers that they will bring the matter to the CEO's attention, and then—and this is the most important step—immediately inform the CEO. My predecessor completely missed the importance of establishing himself as **the** key leader in the organization, through whom all proper communication and collaboration flowed. Instead, he slavishly deferred to the board on practically all matters great and small, and was oblivious to the informal and mostly improper communications between staff and board.

Board volunteers are, oddly enough, both an internal and an external audience in any nonprofit institution. They are internal in the sense that no nonprofit could legitimately function without them. Their role of protecting the mission, setting the strategic direction, and providing financial support, stewardship and oversight, makes them essential to the identity and sustainability of any nonprofit institution. But as some volunteers have reminded me over the years, they are just that, volunteers, and as such, the real center of their lives lies elsewhere. Even the most dedicated volunteers are both insiders and outsiders, and to the extent that they are outsiders, staff should treat their inquiries—with the exception of the legitimate give and take in, say, a strategic planning meeting—just as they would treat an inquiry from the press: listen, gather whatever information they can, and without comment, refer the matter to the CEO. Internal communication—communication that is purely staff to staff—by contrast should be as unfettered as possible. Every nonprofit institution, every nation, every historical epoch, is moved either backward or forward, is defined as having succeeded or failed, by the quality of its ideas. It is one thing for CEOs to constrain the communications of staff to external audiences; it is quite another to extend those constraints internally. To do so diminishes the number and quality of the ideas of the institution and brings with it the prospect of mediocrity. Staff must have the absolute assurance of the CEO that they can express whatever they have in mind, even if—especially if—it runs counter to the point of view of the CEO. And CEOs must be wise enough to know when the ideas of others trump their own. When nonprofit CEOs are truly leading their organizations, and the only way truly to lead is to lead with ideas, they must be willing, modestly and graciously, to accept the judgment of staff that an idea of theirs simply will not work. Ideas are central to the success of any organization, and the CEOs who create a climate in which ideas flow freely have the best chance of succeeding, that is, of course, if they can master the political dimensions of their nonprofit institutions. And what could be more political than an annual meeting?

The Vagaries of Succession

Presidential successions are very often
like Russian roulette:
potentially deadly to the CEO
and to the institution itself.

An annual meeting, a seemingly perfunctory event, very often has profound political implications. My first annual meeting as the CEO of the organization did indeed have moments both perfunctory and profound. For perfunctories there was a pre-dinner reception followed by an undistinguished chicken dinner, a call to order, a financial report by the board treasurer, and my state of the union (though it was mostly disunion) address in which our little successes were invoked and our larger failures ignored. This was followed by a performance by our youth dance troupe, three award presentations for board service, and a Youth of the Year speech. Then it was time for the profundities: Tommy DiTullio's nominating report, and the remarks of the incoming president, Greg Robertson.

Tommy, who was actually quite good on his feet if he had a couple of glasses of wine beforehand, was on this night embarrassingly bad. He had obviously had more wine than his customary two glasses, because the moment he was introduced he let out a loud cackle that could be heard above the applause of the crowd. Tommy's voice that night was artificially loud and deep as if he were mocking the mellifluous voice of a television anchor. Perhaps it was prophetic that he mispronounced the word unanimous—changing the second n to an m, so that it came out unaminous—because the unanimous, and perfunctory, vote taken that night would have a profound effect on me and on the future of the organization. The vote renominated several board volunteers whose terms should have been allowed to expire quietly and uneventfully, including Tommy's old colleague from City Hall, Maria DiSanto, and it brought onto the board Bobby Hathaway and promoted one of Tommy's friends, Larry Miller, to an officer position. Greg Robertson's remarks, after he was formally elected president of the organization, were kept for last.

In retrospect I should have had our Youth of the Year, who gave a very moving speech about how the organization had helped him, speak last—and in future years I would do just that—but in deference to the incoming president of the board, I scheduled Greg to go last. Because our dance troupe had performed late in the program, the spotlight that was used for their performance was still pointed at the podium in the front of the ballroom. The man who stepped into this bright orb of light, the silver-haired if not silver-tongued Greg Robertson, did so with a dignity more in keeping with some high office than the presidency of a nonprofit. Greg had obviously heard other Youths of the Year speak, because in a formal speech that lasted about thirty minutes he told his life story from his tragic childhood to his not inconsiderable success in the insurance business. He began to sweat as he spoke, his complexion transforming from florid to ashen gray. His performance and his demeanor made me wonder if perhaps he was ill or inordinately nervous and made me think, on a more philosophical level, about the vagaries of presidential successions, which, regardless of how well they are vetted or how well they are orchestrated (with Greg I did not have the opportunity to do either), are very often like Russian roulette: potentially deadly to the CEO and to the institution itself. Somehow Greg managed to finish the speech, but what I realized, and what others there that night confirmed to me, was that I now had a president who lacked the fundamental attribute of leadership: a sense of proportion. And though I did not need any further confirmation of this fact, I got it the next morning when Greg called Meg Michalski and announced to her, "Now that I am in charge, I want you to…" And then proceeded to tell her what he wanted her to do.

Meg Michalski rushed into my office, visibly shaken. "Greg Robertson just called," and she told me verbatim everything that Greg had told her. "Should I do what he told me to do?"

"Meg, who do you work for?"

"I work for you."

"That's right," I said, "and I work for them. So I'll handle this."

I called Greg immediately, and he agreed to meet me for lunch. The very next thing I did was to call my old friend and mentor, Patrick McSweeney, a man who, if he was not born politically astute, as a Boston-born Irishman certainly had it thrust upon him. Patrick and I met while I was working for the international organization in New York. I eventually recruited him to serve on a international committee for which I had leadership responsibility. We immediately connected on a number of levels—social, political and intellectual. Patrick introduced me to the pleasures of scotch on-the-rocks and the fascinating world of organizational politics. I brought to the friendship an eagerness to learn; and a love of history and literature and philosophy, all of which appealed to my Jesuit-educated friend. We had already spent many nights—sometimes the whole night, during a conference or after a committee meeting—talking about the business we were in and its political dynamics or just reflecting on matters more intellectual, like whether Gladstone was right when he said that all one needed to know to be educated for leadership was contained in Homer, in **The Iliad** and **The Odyssey**. And wisdom was what I needed at the moment, whether it came from the ancient world or the political genius of Patrick McSweeney.

"I think with this guy," Patrick said, "you might have to talk to some of your Sicilian friends about mixing up a nice pair of cement shoes."

"I think I might need more than one pair," I said.

"This guy Robertson obviously has no idea of what his role is as a board volunteer, let alone a board president," Patrick said.

"Maybe I should have you come in and do some kind of board retreat," I said.

"Not a bad idea. But your immediate problem is your lunch meeting with this guy. You need to get his attention. Or I should say, you need to divert his attention away from trying to manage the organization. You've told me that the organization has a very limited endowment, right? So what you do is persuade this guy that his legacy lies with establishing an endowment for the Agency. It's all about legacy with these people, about fame and fortune, about being remembered after they're gone."

"Vapory fame," I said, "is what Marcus Aurelius called it."

"So give this guy some vapor, puff him up

a bit."

I tried to do just that: puff Greg up a bit at lunch that day. "I don't want to see you get bogged down in the quotidian details of the organization" I told him at one point. "As the board president, I want you to be able to keep your eye on the big picture of the organization."

"How are you defining the big picture?" Greg asked.

What I needed at that moment was a grand vision of the organization, which, after a year of reorientation and reorganization, had yet to be forged. That vision, which is so important to any organization, would crystallize later, but not until I stepped back on the international stage as a member of the international organization's strategic planning commission. For the moment, I had to rely on that other institutional verity: our mission.

"I see the mission as the big picture," I said, "and I see you as the key person to articulate it and protect it."

"Mission is important," he conceded, "but I don't think protecting the mission is enough for a president to do."

And with that remark I had the opening I

needed. "You're absolutely right," I said. "As the president of the organization, you need something big, a big idea, to command your attention, something to ensure that this organization will endure, financially and otherwise, long after we're gone."

There it was: a nod to Lincoln, and whether a nation, or in this case a nonprofit institution, can long endure and a nod to the insurance mogul's preoccupation with financial security.

And Greg, a smart (if somewhat out of kilter) guy, got my drift. "We do need long-term financial security," he said. "What we need is an endowment."

Bingo! Patrick McSweeney, I thought, you're a genius.

"I wholeheartedly agree," I said. "And you're the perfect person to get it done, Greg"

"I don't know about that," he said, his self-satisfied smile betraying a false modesty.

"No, your assessment is spot on. That's exactly where we need to go, and you're the perfect person to lead us there."

As I left Greg Robertson that afternoon I thought that our lunch could not have gone any better. Greg had the big project I wanted him to have, a project that could command his entire attention during his two-year tenure as president, and best of all, it was his idea, not mine. But my small triumph lasted less than a week when Greg called to tell me that, in view of what he called "the AIDS epidemic," we needed a blood-borne pathogens policy. The policy he wanted us to adopt was literally a volume; it was about ten times the size of our entire personnel handbook. We convened a personnel committee meeting at which Greg stood up at one point to make a passionate plea for his blood-borne pathogens policy. Luckily there was no real support for what he was proposing, with virtually everyone on the committee preferring a modestly proportioned two-or three-sentence policy statement. Even without any committee support, Greg seemed determined to carry the fight to the full board. He quickly abandoned that course of action when an unforeseen and unfortunate crisis came to command his undivided attention. When a fatal injury to one of our kids resulted in a lawsuit against the organization, Greg became a kind of self-appointed investigator of the incident, visiting the scene of the accident again and again, interviewing and re-interviewing staff, particularly Evelyn Wagner, on whom he seemed to place the blame for what was clearly an accident. The implication was that, if Matt Mihalak had been in charge of the Agency's overall program instead of Evelyn Wagner, the accident never would have happened. If the accident was avoidable—and there was no evidence, however determined Greg Robertson was to find it, that negligence was involved—it seemed to me that Howard Sinden was the staff person who could have avoided it.

As soon as we received the first inquiry from the press regarding the accident, I quickly pulled together a crisis management team that included me, the officers of the board, and two other board members: an attorney and a public relations executive. Then we drafted a brief opening statement and agreed that I would be the press spokesman. In most organizations, these decisions are made and put in writing under the rubric of a crisis management plan long before any crisis occurs. Either way, the key is to move quickly, pick a spokesperson, and take the initiative.

I was not at all sure what motivated the members of the committee to have me act as the spokesman for the organization. Was it good judgment or simply self-protection? Whatever their motivation was that day, I have on reflection concluded that a good CEO should aggressively seek to play the role of spokesperson in a crisis, that is, of course, if one has the temperament to stay calm in a crisis and if one truly believes one has the wisdom to sort out the competing ethical and political obligations. It is never easy to sort out competing obligations, especially in a crisis, when political concerns pull you to protect the organization and its reputation, while ethical obligations demand a truthfulness that could put the organization's reputation in jeopardy. The thing to remember in any crisis is this: if the public relations people want you to spin the truth and the lawyers want you to parse the truth, it is your obligation, straightforwardly and unequivocally, to tell the truth. The truth ultimately comes out anyway, and it is better that you, as the executive leader of the institution, are the first to tell it.

If Greg Robertson had been angling for a fight with the full board over a bizarre bloodborne pathogens policy, I suspected him to be even more pugnacious about the lawsuit that had been lodged against us. My suspicion seemed to be confirmed when I did not hear anything from Greg regarding the agenda for the upcoming board meeting.

The first thing I noticed when that fateful board meeting was called to order was that every single member of the board but one was there that day. A majority of board members always attended board meetings, but having almost everyone there only happened one other time in my tenure: the day the board had to vote on whether to exonerate me or let me go. Like the curious who gather at the scene of an accident, there was an anxious air of expectancy in the boardroom that day, as if something volcanic were about to erupt. Everyone seemed to sense, as they nervously glanced at one another, that the source of that potential eruption was the mercurial man seated at the head of the table, Greg Robertson. After calling the meeting to order, a calmness came over Greg that I had not seen before. Rather than launch an attack, which I expected him to do, he quietly read from a prepared statement. I was seated close enough to Greg to see that his statement was handwritten and liberally edited. He had obviously labored over it. The whole statement, except for the very last line, was a reflection on his many years of involvement in the organization, reaching back to his fond boyhood memories of learning to swim in the organization's pool all the way up to how proud he was to be elected president of the organization. It was clear to me and everyone else in the room that Greg was going to resign as the president of the board. But we were stunned by the announcement anyway, and everyone fell silent for a moment, quickly followed by a polite, respectful, and I would have to say—even among Greg's allies on the board—relieved applause.

A few days later I received another letter of resignation, this time from the president-elect, Diandra Gray. These resignations (Peter Matthews's would come later) completed a process of change that removed an entire faction—or so I thought—from its position of power in the organization and opened an opportunity to rebuild the board. Greg Robertson's resignation in particular removed what would have been a very troubled presidency to manage. And with almost all the key staff positions ready to be reconstituted, I had a very real opportunity to reshape the entire organization. But reshaping it would take wisdom and luck, patience and political acumen.

And it would take time. The reshaping of the organization would take years rather than months, and while it unfolded an opportunity presented itself for me to step on the national stage again. After a long absence without any national involvement, I accepted an invitation to serve on the international organization's Commission for the 21st Century. After being bogged down by organizational in-fighting and petty politics, it was liberating to think that I could turn my attention to forging a vision for my own organization and for our entire international federation.

2

Strategy

A fox knows many things, a hedgehog one big thing.
~Archilochus

They could see with great exactness,
But at no great distance.
~Jonathon Swift

Strategic Thinking

Strategic thinking does not proceed
in a straight line from A to B;
it is instead a journey about the texture of the line.

I had been on strategic planning teams before, both at an international and local level, but none of my past experiences proved to be as profound as this one. I came away from this experience with a much deeper understanding of the difference between strategic planning and strategic thinking and of the seeming inevitability of mission creep. I came away realizing that it is extraordinarily difficult to forge a grand vision that is commensurate with an historic mission. And I came away realizing that big ideas are very often the first casualty of strategic planning.

We gathered for the first time in the ballroom of a New York City hotel, about sixty of us, representing every region of the U.S. and some of our international affiliates. There were international board volunteers and local board volunteers, international staff and CEOs of local organizations. Anne Hopkins, an international board member from San Francisco, served as chair of the Commission. In her welcoming remarks, which opened the three-day session, she reminded everyone that this was only the third Commission in the almost one hundred year history of the international organization. Actually there had been many strategic planning groups over the years: this group happened to be the third one to have the more elevated title of Commission. Anne Hopkins's message that day was that we had very important work to do in advocating for young people and continuing to reach out to underserved youth. I wondered to what extent the call to continued growth would be taken up by the keynote speaker that day, the international president, Eileen Boyer.

Eileen Boyer and I were first introduced in the early eighties when the director of the program department hired me to work as a program specialist at the international headquarters in New York. I did not meet Eileen, the assistant director of the program department and my direct supervisor, until my first day on the job. Eileen had inherited me, and she did not seem particularly pleased to have done so. Tough-minded and talented, a workaholic with a laser-sharp, analytical mind, Eileen was poised to rise in a corporate bureaucracy that I found constraining and politically petty. By the time I left the international organization several years later to return to the more congenial position of CEO of a local organization, Eileen had become the department director, then, shortly after that, senior vice-president, and finally president of the international organization. Our relationship, forged in the high pressure environment of international headquarters—an environment in which crises were routinely contrived—deepened over time to a close friendship marked by mutual respect and admiration: Eileen for what she has always regarded as my depth of thought and I for her intellect, her heart, and her implacable spirit.

On a cold January day in the comfortable confines of a busy New York hotel, Eileen keynoted our deliberations in a way that marked a new departure for her. Ordinarily Eileen's public remarks were models of logical, linear thought, with a sprinkling of platitudes. She would typically start slowly, her voice shallow and breathy, then get into a commanding rhythm before tying everything together into a neat, factual knot. Her remarks that day, more philosophical than practical, more visionary than analytical, were a perfect opening to the larger question of where we were headed in our second century on the youth development scene. Or perhaps I should say where we were headed on the world scene because Eileen staked out a claim for us to produce not just good citizens in our respective communities, but citizens of the world. In asking the philosophical questions of who we are and why we exist, she was positing the idea that our institution was potentially an agent of change on a grand scale, that we had a responsibility to America and to the world to shape the next generation into citizens of the world, citizens capable of changing their communities, changing America, changing the world. We lived in a global society, she argued, one bound by a common humanity. It would fall to us to prepare the nearly five million kids we served to function effectively in that global society and to change it for the better. But to do that, she said, we would have to be much more intentional about instilling a sense of civic responsibility in our kids, a goal which had always been implicit in our mission but now needed to be made explicit. The grand vision of an enlightened generation notwithstanding, she could not help but mention a more mundane matter: the need, with so many impending retirements, to develop a whole new generation of CEOs. Still, she had a vision, a grand vision if you will, of the future. What she did not have was the rhetoric to match it. The rhetoric would come from a speech I would write for her, which she delivered at our international conference later that year.

After Eileen's inspirational remarks, David Stewart, our facilitator, took what could only be called complete command of the proceedings. David had once been one of only two assistant international directors of our organization, a brilliant young guy whose rise was so quick that he seemed to be headed for the international presidency in his thirties. His meteoric rise was knocked off course by our other assistant international director, a man of less intellect perhaps but considerably more political acumen. David Stewart was perceptive enough to realize that he was being outdistanced politically and he left the organization in the mid eighties to found what would become an extraordinarily successful consulting firm.

When I went to the international organization in the eighties, David was already assistant international director in charge of several departments, including mine, program. I admired him greatly. He was brilliant, he set very high expectations for all of us, and no one, not even Eileen Boyer, worked harder than David Stewart. He was also a manic man given to contriving crises. Since everything was of the highest importance to David, even the most quotidian detail, I came to see him as someone who lacked a sense of proportion. He was not, all things considered, the greatest of managers. But as I would soon find out, he was absolutely brilliant at facilitating a strategic planning process. In my experience most facilitators approached strategic planning as if it were a pro forma process, a set sequence of questions to be answered by the group, one after the other. With David Stewart the whole experience was more of an art than a process. It reminded me of one of Coleridge's observations about the poetic process, which he thought began with a God-like apprehension of the whole, followed by what Coleridge called separating "its distinguishable parts," after which "we must restore them in our conceptions to the unity." I do not know about the God-like apprehension part, except that both David and Eileen saw us as an institution poised to promote civic engagement on a grand scale, but analyzing the distinguishable parts is indeed the first major step in any strategic planning process, followed by a unifying synthesis, which is where management experts like Henry Mintzberg believe one does the real poetry, the real strategic thinking. The synthesis, the point at which one finds the pattern, the missing element, the big idea, is intuitive not analytical, with an eye to the future rather than the present or the past.

David's approach was also philosophical in this sense: to the extent that he saw strategic planning as a process, he saw it as a very messy undertaking driven by questions, even uncomfortable questions, some ultimately unanswerable. For David Stewart, strategic thinking does not proceed in a straight line from A to B; it is instead a journey about the texture of the line. And that texture is largely about the two or three big ideas that are truly important. For that is how the corporate headquarters of a federation leads, by compelling ideas, by what Jim Collins calls a Big Hairy Audacious Goal, or BHAG. A corporate headquarters also leads by its values, its core beliefs, and its mission, all of which should remain, in Collins's view, immutable.

The rest of David Stewart's opening remarks revolved around his observation that we had reached a critical threshold in our history as an organization. As a result of two decades of aggressive growth, we were now of sufficient size and scale and we commanded enough respect and attention to take on a BHAG of considerable proportions. But it would not be easy. Our staff turnover among part-time employees was high. Only three per cent of our operating revenues were coming from investments. The non-profit environment was becoming increasingly complex with ever greater demands for accountability. Only one-third of Americans had a high level of trust in non-profits, with most Americans feeling that non-profits were grossly inefficient. But as David pointed out, efficiency, though important, is not a critical factor in assessing the value of non-profits because non-profits build something of compensatory value—social capital and in our case, as a youth development agency—human capital.

It was clear from listening to David Stewart that our rapid growth had in large part brought us to a critical threshold of international respect and attention. The foundation of that growth could be found in our ability to attract and create M&M's: money and marketing. We attracted large sums of money, particularly from federal and state government, but also from corporate America, while we created a recognizable brand. This success was not without its unintended consequences. The most obvious consequence was how would we sustain the growth with many of our senior CEOs close to retirement? And how would we continue to attract board volunteers in an environment in which non-profits were proliferating at an accelerating rate? But the most fundamental question was this: would growth, however effective it was in extending our reach and raising our stature, have an impact on that immutable idea on which our institution was founded, our mission?

Changing the Core

We allowed growth to redefine our mission instead of having mission define our growth.

In the two years it took to complete the strategic plan, a period in which we had three extended meetings, numerous conference calls and many town hall meetings to test our preliminary findings, there were many debates but none more spirited than the one surrounding our mission as an organization. Although it had undergone minor revision in recent decades, our mission had remained essentially the same for more than a century: the development of children from disadvantaged circumstances into productive adults.

Our mission became in part a function of where we were located. Our kids were street kids. They were not typically involved in Scouts, nor were they paying members of the YMCA. In my hometown the Youth Association clubhouse was opened in 1895 by a group of women who saw the need to get the "newsies" off the streets of the downtown commercial district. The "newsies" were young boys who peddled their newspapers downtown and in other parts of the city. Most of them were the sons of Russian, Polish and Italian immigrants, who, when they were not selling their papers, were annoying or harassing the downtown merchants. The Youth Association of that era—and for most of the 20th century—was not on main street in small town American, but on mean street in urban America. Later it would go international, but location, to a large extent, had defined our mission, and our mission, until recently, had defined us.

The earliest mission statement, which was drafted in the first decade of the 20th century, placed us in an urban setting: "The primary mission of the Youth Association is to ensure and enhance the quality of life for boys as participating members of a richly diverse urban society." This early mission statement also stressed the importance of adult guidance—a core principle actually—in helping kids "grow into contributing human beings with the necessary skills for living." By the 1980s our mission statement was distilled down to helping "youth of all backgrounds, with a special concern for those from disadvantaged circumstances, to develop the qualities needed to become responsible citizens and leaders." Our entire history to this point had aligned us, nobly I thought, with the poor and the dispossessed. We were thus aligned because we were always clear about just what the driving force of the institution was: our mission. But by challenging us to revisit that historic mission in the context of a strategic planning process, I discovered that growth, and the money and marketing that supported it, was now the driving force of the institution, and had been for two decades or more. Our debates about the mission, at our Commission meetings and at town hall meetings all across the country, persuaded me that this historic shift had indeed occurred.

I vividly recall a debate at one of our Commission meetings that turned on exchanges between me and two members of the international board of governors: Harold Wressell and Joe Tomassi. The debate took place near the end of the first year of our deliberations when the Commission and the entire Youth Association field were vacillating between essentially two versions of the mission statement. The first version, the one consistent with our historic mission, read: "To inspire and enable all young people, especially those from disadvantaged circumstances, to realize their full potential as productive, responsible and caring citizens." The second version, which confirmed a shift that had already occurred in the minds of many, read: "To provide hope and opportunity for ALL young people, especially those who need us most, so they can reach their full potential as responsible and caring citizens."

Joe Tomassi, the founder of an international fast-food chain and an astute marketing man, was particularly fond of the phrase "hope and opportunity." "I think that phrase could stand alone as our mission statement," he said. "A mission statement should be concise enough so that someone, especially someone who is a board member, can say it in one breath in the time it takes an elevator to go from one floor to another. It should be something as simple as: our mission is to create hope and opportunity for kids. What is that, ten words?" Joe's proposal was met by a chorus of no's from several people seated at my table, one of whom added, "You have to have the word **all** in there."

"Okay," Joe Tomassi conceded, "eleven words."

I personally liked the concision of Joe's mission statement, and although hope and opportunity had a felicitous tone, the phrasing sounded more like a marketing theme than a mission statement. "Joe," I said, "you make a good point, shorter would clearly be better, but I don't think it really works as a mission statement. Someone is bound to ask, where's the beef?"

"Well the way the mission now reads," Joe said, "you have to get through the beef and the potatoes and the dessert to get all the verbiage across to somebody, and as a result, most of us simply don't do it, and the mission doesn't get expressed at all. So I say let's just leave it at creating hope and opportunity for kids."

"**All** kids," the chorus chimed in again.

"But there's no ultimate outcome, no productive and engaged citizen, in just creating hope and opportunity," I said.

"We can't ultimately guarantee that outcome anyway," Joe countered.

"But we can and ought to aspire to it, which is precisely what we have done throughout our history," I said.

"You make a good point," Joe said, "but I still think that if we don't talk the mission, and many of us don't for the reasons I've already expressed, then we won't walk it very well either. We need something more concise, something that's easier to say."

"I agree," I said. "But I don't agree with this emphasis on serving all kids. That's not our mission."

"So you would exclude kids just because they're not disadvantaged?" Harold Wressell, who was seated at my table, said to me as part of a small group discussion about our mission.

My answer to Harold Wressell made this distinction: "If a middle class kid, say, with all kinds of advantages, shows up at the door, I would certainly serve that kid. What I wouldn't do, simply to satisfy some growth goal, is go looking for that kid. I wouldn't move the door to his neighborhood, though that's precisely what we've been doing willy-nilly. What we should do, and have done since our founding, is have a primary concern for kids from disadvantaged circumstances."

"Why not serve both?" Harold said. "Why see one as excluding the other?"

"Because trying to do both is trying to be all things to all people, which doesn't differentiate us from anybody. If our mission is to help all kids become productive citizens, which is"—I did a quick count in my head—"ten words, by the way, that mission could be the Scouts, the Y or any other youth agency. We would lose our identity."

"Maybe that middle class kid has problems, too," Harold said. "Maybe he's at risk and needs our help, too."

"Maybe he is," I said. "But he doesn't need us as much as the kid who is living in poverty and has only one parent."

"But he does need us; you're conceding that much."

"What I'm conceding is that that kid might need the Scouts or the Y or a little more attention from a parent or a teacher."

"It's still not clear to me why we can't serve both kids," John said.

"Again, I think we should serve any kid who shows up at our door. I just don't think that we should grow by moving into middle class suburban neighborhoods. But the data we received now show that one-third of our Clubs are now in suburban areas. We have a little more than two million youth members, with roughly half of those kids living in poverty. Yet in American today, and you saw the data, there are almost twelve million kids living in poverty. That's our market. As we continue to grow, our growth should be into areas where those kids live, kids from disadvantaged circumstances. That's our mission; at least it was our mission, and it was the thing that distinguished us from everybody else."

The chorus came to Harold Wressell's aid, as one of them observed: "That whole disadvantaged thing, though. I think we need to get away from that. It stigmatizes kids."

"No one is calling a kid disadvantaged," I said. "All our mission says is that these kids come from disadvantaged circumstances. Poverty is a circumstance for which a kid bears no responsibility, other than to rise to the challenge to overcome it. The demographer Harold Hodgskinson, whom you may remember spoke at one of our conferences, said that poverty is the most reliable predictor of failure. That has always been our mission, and it's a noble one, as timely now as it was more than a century ago, to help kids from disadvantages circumstances succeed."

"Can't we accomplish the same thing by getting rid of disadvantaged and replacing it with the phrase 'the kids who need us most'?" Harold said. "Doesn't that say the same thing without offending those folks who don't like the term disadvantaged?"

"Harold, however politically appealing that compromise might be, the phrase 'the kids who need us most' can mean anything anybody wants it to mean, it's such a vague generality. And when you add the adjective **all** in there, which some of us not only want in there, but highlighted, we're simply admitting the fact that we allowed growth to redefine our mission, instead of having mission define our growth."

The Strategic Planning Commission's final recommendation to our federation's International Council (the governing body of our organization) was a mission statement that included the word all but did not highlight it, and removed the phrase "from disadvantaged circumstances" and replaced it with the indeterminate "those who need us most." This turn of events was as revealing as it was disappointing. It demonstrated one of the fundamental paradoxes of strategic planning: that growth, a driving force of almost all strategic plans, can become the driving force of the institution itself. Over a twenty-five year period, but especially in the last decade, our international organization became so successful at fundraising and the marketing strategies to support it, that money and marketing began to drive growth, and growth in turn began to drive the institution itself. If mission had been driving the institution, as it should have been, it would have guided our growth to kids who truly needed us most, kids from disadvantaged circumstances. Instead we allowed growth to redefine our mission by attenuating our commitment to kids from disadvantaged circumstances. We shifted our commitment from the mean streets to main street, from kids with dire disadvantages to all kids, from a market niche to no niche at all. If this shift seemed subtle to some—after all, they argued, what is the difference between kids from disadvantaged circumstances and the kids who need us most?—it was absolutely fundamental to me. It meant we were no longer a mission driven institution. And the tragedy was that most of the people on the Commission and most of the people in our field did not even know it. Most of them could not remember a time, as I and some others could, when money and marketing and growth were not center stage.

But no one could say we were not warned about being too preoccupied with money. No one could say we were not cautioned about letting the acquisition of wealth lead us where it may. We were warned by Jim Collins, one of the wisest business observers in America today. Collins addressed almost three thousand of us at an international conference before the Commission for the 21st Century was formed. He was unequivocal about warning us not to chase money. In Collins' view, the money we need, and certainly all nonprofit institutions need money, should be guided by mission, core values, and ambitious goals. For Collins a great company is guided by the belief that its mission and core values should remain constant, whereas everything else—procedures, policies, strategies—is subject to change. A great company, a visionary company "carefully preserves and protects its core ideology, yet all the specific manifestations of its core ideology must be open for change and evolution."

We were obviously tinkering with our core ideology. We changed our mission, and we changed some of our core values, dropping some, adding others, and rewriting still others to give them a different emphasis. Apparently it was no longer necessary to have affordability as a core value. Low dues had always been a core value so that kids from disadvantaged circumstances—i.e., kids living in poverty—could afford it. The emerging emphasis to serve all kids made affordability unnecessary, even undesirable in some places. And while we dropped affordability, we added two new core values: recognition, and raising the expectations of children. These two values had long been strategies under the core value of behavioral guidance, which also was dropped, even though it went to the core of our identity as a guidance and youth development institution. Changing the core was only part of our repudiation of the Collins business model. While the Commission was changing the core of the institution, the international organization was busy formalizing and institutionalizing policies and standards which were peripheral to the core mission and values. Oddly, incongruously, we were in the process of turning the Collins' model upside down. While we were changing the core, we were trying to preserve everything else, and in so doing, we were becoming what Collins called foxes instead of the preferred metaphor of hedgehogs.

Foxes and Hedgehogs

The hedgehog takes the complexity of the world and simplifies it into a unifying principle, into one big idea.
~Jim Collins

For Jim Collins, one of the key questions any institution must ask itself is whether it is a fox or a hedgehog. The idea behind the question comes from his inexhaustible research, but he took the metaphor to describe it from a famous essay by Isaiah Berlin in which Berlin divided the literary world into foxes and hedgehogs. In Berlin's literary landscape, Plato, who had a controlling vision that pervaded his work, was a hedgehog, whereas Shakespeare, who had many brilliant insights into human nature but no discernible philosophy, was a fox. Berlin took the metaphor for his essay from the ancient Greek poet Archilochus who wrote that "the fox knows many things, but the hedgehog knows one big thing." And just as in human nature, where the cunning and fleet-footed fox attempts but always fails to overtake the plodding and porcupined hedgehog—the fox fails because at the crucial moment the hedgehog rolls up into a ball of spikes and foils the attack—businesses that succeed, businesses that dare to be great, are almost always hedgehogs. The hedgehog takes the complexity of the world and simplifies it into a unifying principle, into one big idea. The fox's effort is not nearly as concentrated. It sees the world in all its complexity, and rather than reshape the many paths of life into one, it pursues many paths simultaneously. Unfortunately, the fox sees the world as our international organization had come to see it: complex and diffuse.

David Stewart, who was fond of quoting Jim Collins, but also Tocqueville and Martin Buber and many others, challenged us as Commission members to identify what our hedgehog concept was. He put us into small groups and had each group report out. A number of ideas were advanced as possibilities, but none resonated with the entire group. The hedgehog discussion was—momentarily, I thought—set aside. David, in his wisdom, very often discussed things out of sequence, brilliantly bringing them together later. I thought the hedgehog idea would certainly be brought back into the discussion, but despite a couple of attempts on my part, it was dropped altogether. I may have been the only Commission member other than our facilitator who wanted to pursue the hedgehog idea. I think the reason there were no other hedgehogs among us was that, whatever we might have thought about a world of work defined by hedgehogs and foxes, most of us had already been converted into foxes by our international organization. This conversion had come about in part because of the international organization's fascination with standards, which we called Standards of Organizational Effectiveness or SOE's.

Our organization had always had operating standards, but until relatively recently there were only a handful of them. A list of those standards would not even have filled a page. For practically all of our history a few rather than many standards were what guided us. In that sense we had always inclined more to the hedgehog idea of finding simplicity where others found complexity. Two things happened to change that perspective: Enron, to which our national organization and the political class in Washington overreacted, and an increasing fascination by our international organization with everything analytical. The overreaction led the international organization to take off the shelf a seldom-used self evaluation model appropriately titled Standards of Self

Evaluation and merge it with the Standards of Organizational Effectiveness. The evaluation model, which had more than a hundred statements in it, had been used voluntarily by local organizations. Some local organizations used the Standards of Self Evaluation simply as a way of periodically—usually every three years—doing an overall evaluation of the organization. Others used it to gather information which could then be used as a part of a strategic planning process. There were others who did not use it at all. But in light of Enron and other scandals and a persistent preoccupation with analytical models in general, the two models were merged, refined, and expanded to as many as 250 standards.

This new model was now known simply as the SOE's, the Standards of Organizational Effectiveness. More importantly, the SOE's later became requirements of membership by a vote of our International Council. Suddenly we had gone from a federation with a few fundamental standards to one obligating us to comply with literally hundreds of them. It is not entirely clear what local organizations (all of which have one vote in the International Council) actually voted to make the SOE's a requirement of membership. There seems to be no record of what organizations constituted the quorum and what organizations actually voted. One of Tocqueville's great admonishments had to do with the tyranny of the majority. The institutionalization of the SOE's may go down as an even stranger exercise in democracy: a tyranny of the minority.

Aside from having the effect of attenuating a once proud tradition of local autonomy, institutionalizing the SOE's ended any chance of finding that elusive hedgehog concept. Our attention would henceforth be concentrated on the quotidian detail rather than the grand sweep, on the tactical rather than the strategic. The reaction in the field to the passage of the SOE's as requirements of membership was mixed. A few of my colleagues around the country resented it; many more were resigned to it; and others like Ed Swoger, the CEO of a big Midwest affiliate, were firm believers in the value that SOE's added to local organizations. When the subject of the SOE's came up at one of Eileen Boyer's international advisory council meetings—a council of twenty local CEOs serving at the pleasure of the international president—Ed Swoger and I had an extended exchange on the topic. The exchange began after I made the observation that the SOE's were more of a distraction than anything else, and they would do more harm than good.

Ed, who was one of the most intelligent and respected CEOs in our field, said, "How can you say that? It's one of the best tools we have."

"If trying to pay attention to 250 things is not a distraction, I don't know what is?"

"No one is saying you have to pay attention to 250 things. It's just a tool to help you assess what **is** important."

"Important to whom?" I said. "We just went through the SOE process with our board and field service staff from our regional office. After field service went back and analyzed it, they came back with eight things they wanted us to do. They wanted another plan for this and another plan for that. What's important to us right now, what's really commanding our attention, is a capital campaign to build a new building. Of the eight things the national organization wanted us to? Maybe **one** is worth doing."

"Then just do that one thing," Ed said.

"And mess up the work plan of my regional service director? It's in his work plan to get those eight things accomplished. That's how he gets evaluated. Over time, he's going to come to me and say, Michael, I need this and I need that. We're not the customer anymore, Ed. They're not meeting our needs. We're meeting theirs. They're the customer."

Although Ed Swoger continued to be calm, his normally ruddy face got a little redder. "What is it you think you need then?"

"I need not to be distracted by all this quotidian detail, which makes it much more difficult to think strategically. Getting stuck in all this analytical detail makes it much more difficult for me to concentrate on the big ideas, to concentrate on a vision of the future. I need to be able to think strategically. I've heard more than one of our colleagues say the SOE's are great because they make a strategic plan unnecessary."

"I don't agree with that. I think you need a strategic plan. But I also think you need standards, and when I show the SOE document to funders and others in our community, they are impressed by the fact that we are an organization with high standards."

"That's fine, Ed. We can still have this tool, as you like to call it, but not make every one of the 250 standards in it, requirements for membership in our international organization. I think there are ten or twelve standards that ought to be requirements of membership, and the rest can remain in the document, which you can still show all those funders in your town. Instead we should use the SOE's as a reference tool, and as a mechanism for gathering internal information prior to a strategic planning process. That's how I think this document should be used."

"I'm just afraid that it's the rigorousness of the standards that's really bothering you. I think we need to have more rigor in our standards, particularly with all this growth and all these new CEOs who will really benefit from a tool like this. You may not need it, Michael, but they do. And we all need standards more than ever because of increasing concerns about ethics."

Since no one said anything to support my position on this issue, I was left with the impression that Ed Swoger had won the argument about the relative merits of the Standards of Organizational Effectiveness. Later, and only confidentially, a sizeable number of CEOs there that day expressed to me their agreement with many of my criticisms of the SOE's, but they did not want to say any of those things in front of Eileen Boyer, whom they all respected and feared in varying degrees; respected because of her keen intellect and her considerable accomplishments as national president; and feared because she could at times be formidable, unmovable, even unapproachable, but never, like some of her predecessors, vindictive.

Regardless of my respect for Eileen's analytical ability and for Ed Swoger's adroit analysis, I thought that they and many others in our movement were wrong in their assessment of the value and the long-term effect of an analytical model like the SOE's. If the standards movement had initially brought value and credibility to nonprofit world, it had over time become a bureaucratic bane, transforming that which was original and vital in organizations like ours into a bureaucratized, sanitized, overly centralized cookie-cutter institution. By pushing the idea of standards too far, the SOE's ushered in an era of management by checklist instead of strategic vision. This new era of supposed high standards was one in which art gave way to craft, in which painting with originality devolved into a humdrum task of painting by the numbers. So not only did we all become foxes, we became not even very original ones at that.

And to what did we owe this bureaucratic devolution? We owed it to unbridled growth and to the eventual shift away from local autonomy to command and control from our international organization. The shift in power and influence from local to international, from a decentralized governance model to a more centralized one, ironically occurred at time when the rest of the world was actually decentralizing, or flattening, as Tom Friedman characterized it in his brilliant book **The World Is Flat**. Apparently the many new CEOs and other staff coming into our organization believed needed cookie-cutter models to operate effectively. They believed we were, as that wonderfully platitudinous and fallacious phrase would have it, only as good as our weakest link.

Along with growth came a recognizable brand, and once the brand was built, it had to be protected. To protect the brand one presumably needed more standardization, thus more centralization. Standards were like rules, and our philosophy was, the more the better. Instead of the dozen operating standards that had served us well for decades, it was better to have 250. Instead of being guided by five ideas to have a positive impact on the kids we served, which is what our current research initially revealed, it was better to expand that number into an impact model with 365 standard statements. And with all these standards—and there would be many more as a result of future forays into ethics and executive development—came the clarion call for metrics, the other commandment of the accountability crowd. Accountability was now more important than autonomy. We were accountable to donors, to government, and to the public at large. The only way to assure those publics that we were meeting a proper standard of accountability was to measure it. The way to measure outcomes was to graft metrics onto analytical models like the SOE's and the new impact model. And the only way ultimately to measure the impact a youth agency can have on its clients was to make social science try to do what it cannot do—measure the immeasurable.

Measuring the number of kids we served, even measuring the number who came to our clubhouses on a regular basis, did not prove impact—and these were the hardest numbers we had. Attempts to demonstrate improved school performance or a diminution of contact with juvenile authorities were perhaps more persuasive measures of impact, but they hardly constituted an objective proof either. As for quality standards models like SOEs or the impact model, where teams of staff and board members read and rated standards on a scale of unsatisfactory to excellent, one invariably found the reign of opinion rather than fact. An organization with an excellent rating may not have been excellent at all. It was simply excellent in the opinion of the committee that rated it. Opinion on top of opinion conducing to something measurable—a score of, say, 900, would garner one a rating of excellent—had little to do with social science or the metrics it espoused. The idea that an opinion was measurable was like arguing that astrology and astronomy were equivalent. Neither science nor social science has thus far demonstrated the capacity to render an objective truth about exactly what it is that changes a child's life for the better. The strictly analytical approach of applying quality standards to measure impact has not arrived at any fundamental truth. The protean approach of the fox ultimately led us to diffusion and distraction. What we needed was the concision and single-mindedness of a hedgehog. Once an organization has found its hedgehog concept—the one big idea that sets it apart from any other—then impact becomes clearer.

I have always thought that forging secure attachments between kids and caring adults was indeed our hedgehog concept. Most of the professionals in our movement regard relationship-building as a core value, but one that has tactical not strategic significance. I think my colleagues have a tendency to see the adult-child relationship in tactical terms because other agencies, especially United Ways with their emphasis on measurable outcomes, tend to see the child as a means to a programmatic end, as an outcome. In this view of the child, the adult and the relationship are tactics to arrive at outcomes like improved grades or civil behavior.

The strategic view regards children and their secure attachments to caring adults as ends in themselves. However important it is for children to do well in school and to be civil and decent human beings, these are not, human nature being what it is, universal human longings. But a sense of belonging, forged in the trust and mutual respect of a child's secure attachment to a caring adult—which is compellingly described in David and Beatrix Hamburg's **Learning To Live Together**—is indeed a universal human need. The institution that recognizes this fact and concentrates its talents and resources and strategic energies on it will have a hedgehog concept powerful enough to transform a generation of children. Tragically, amid all our attention to the quotidian and its attendant diffusion of effort, my own institution lacked the leadership to do it. But this was not the only casualty of the Commission, not the only big idea to be lost in the fray. There was the matter of leadership itself—executive leadership.

Strategic Planning

Strategic planning is an oxymoron.

By the third day of the first Commission meeting I began to marvel at David Stewart's deft handling of the dynamics of such a large group. He knew, like no other strategic planner I had ever seen, when to test the group, when to linger on an idea and when summarily to touch on another. If the path we were on seemed labyrinthian at times, if it seemed to go backward when it should have gone forward, David commanded every twist and turn with the aplomb of a pitcher in his prime. His pitches came at us from all angles and at varying speeds. One pitch in particular, which was thrown high and hard as if to challenge us to hit it out of the park, was the question of executive leadership.

"How many A executives do you think we have in our movement right now?" David asked.

There was a hush of people thinking, calculating. Then one of the international organization's senior vice-presidents, Clyde Thompson, a smooth-talking Floridian who was held in high regard by CEOs of local organizations, said, "I'd say about a third."

David crossed his arms, pensive for a moment. "That many?" he said with just a hint of incredulity.

"At least, and very probably more," Clyde Thompson said, displaying that characteristic optimism and southern charm that made him so likable.

David did a quick scan of the room. "You agree with that?"

I could not agree. Nor was I sure of how

many A executives were in our field. I was only sure that it was lower than Clyde's sanguine estimate, but otherwise I was distracted by thoughts of what an A executive actually was. Was it shorthand for a common business term that others in the room understood, but I, an avid reader of the classics and only a casual reader of business books, did not? I would soon learn that it had no such definitive meaning. The international organization would define an A executive on its terms, and I would define it on mine. For the moment, I followed the advice of Epictetus, who drolly observed that since we had two ears and one mouth we should listen twice as much as we talked. I listened.

A local organization CEO concurred with Clyde Thompson. A board volunteer, perhaps emboldened by the CEO's calculation and by Clyde's optimistic estimate, put the number of A executives in our field at forty per cent. Then Eileen Boyer suggested a number I thought more realistic, "I'd put the number at ten per cent," she said; and when no one else was inclined to comment on the A executive issue, David Stewart quickly moved on to something else. The idea of executive development would continue to be discussed by the Commission and would ultimately become a key consideration in our strategic plan, but Eileen's cautious estimate was the last time the term "A executive" received any mention at all. The idea, if not the term, resurfaced a few months later at a meeting of Eileen Boyer's international advisory council. I noticed that executive development was on the agenda sent out prior to the meeting, which prompted me to start reflecting not so much on the number of A's I thought were in our field, but rather on what the idea of an A executive actually meant. I began to see this whole question of the A executive as a potentially big idea with enormous strategic implications for our plan and for our field. I started writing down my thoughts on the subject. Writing my thoughts in a fuller form—not just words and phrases but carefully crafted sentences and paragraphs—always had the salutary effect of clarifying my thinking on any subject. The more I pondered the topic of the A executive, the more I wrote. I filled a small notebook on the strategic possibilities of an A executive program, an abridged version of which I took with me to the international advisory council meeting. When the council's attention turned to the agenda item on executive development, the entire tone of the meeting changed. A sober and business-like tone was quickly replaced by a buzz of excitement and anticipation. I saw people sit up and lean forward. Suddenly there was a kid-in-the-candy-store atmosphere, and in no one was this excitement more palpable than Eileen Boyer, who rarely if ever showed such emotion, and Clyde Thompson, who stood up to introduce the agenda item to the group.

As a presenter Clyde Thompson was smooth and concise, and if not eloquent, articulate. What he described in his introduction was a uniform performance management system for executive development which sounded similar to another analytical system popular with the bureaucratic crowd, the SOE's. The not-so-new system was based on identifying and systematizing skill sets, hard and soft skills, and personal attributes. The assessment would then lead to an individualized performance plan presumably capable of transforming a C executive into a B and a B into an A. "Our CEOs," Clyde concluded, "are the franchise players in our field. They are the ones who can move an organization forward."

I was disconcerted and astonished at what I heard Clyde Thompson say about executive development. I was disconcerted to learn that anything big about the idea of an A executive had already been taken off the strategic table—prematurely and preemptively, I thought. It was a reminder to me that big ideas are always the first casualty of strategic planning, a casualty brought on by a hasty retreat to an analytical position. I was astonished that barely six months into a two-year strategic planning process the question of executive leadership had already been decided, not by the Commission, not by the field as a whole, but by the international staff and a management consulting firm. They had taken the initiative, but they had taken it impetuously and presumptuously.

I had come to the advisory council meeting with perhaps too much to say about the topic, and with roughly twenty other people in the room I realized that I would probably be limited to the equivalent of a couple of soundbites. I took my limited opportunity to say that the performance management system just described was banal and uninspiring. I said that skill sets, a term that Clyde Thompson had used like a mantra, was a trivial way of looking at executive leadership. What we really lacked as an organization, and what the new system with all its quotidian concerns fundamentally failed to address, was not a lack of skill but a dearth of talent. By my own calculation, I thought the number of A executives in our field was considerably less than Eileen's estimate of ten per cent, and more like two or three per cent.

Shortly after the advisory council meeting, the international organization announced the opening of a new position, vice president for executive development, and shortly after that one of Clyde Thompson's protégés from the southern regional office was hired to be the new skill sets guru. Ken Ivie, a very capable but buttoned-downed Southerner with apparently the right skill sets, took on the task of administering the performance management system and of presenting it to the field at a session of our national conference. I sat in the back of a national conference audience of several hundred CEOs and board volunteers as Ken Ivie took the stage flanked by two consultants. Ken capably but disingenuously presented the new program as a work in progress. Actually, most of the work was done, and it was done with the kind of analytical overkill for which our international organization was well known. The system was now comprised of forty-nine skill sets. Maybe some enterprising skill sets enthusiast could come up with a fiftieth skill set, I thought, as we were regaled with a definition of the A executive that was little more than a cobbling together of forty-nine component parts. Finally, the floor was opened for questions. I raised my hand near the end of the question and answer part of the session, and Ken Ivie, who knew that I had objections to the program, graciously acknowledged me.

"I have a comment and a question," I said to Ken, intending my comment for the crowd and my question for him. "We should keep in mind that the program you just described is coming out of a strategic planning process that is still ongoing. We should also keep in mind that strategic planning is, in a sense, an oxymoron. By that I mean, the planning part, which is analytical, has a way of undoing that which was strategic in the first place. Planning can in effect nullify a vision; it can do away with a big idea arrived at by a synthesis rather than an analysis. So my question is, with regard to the executive development program you just described, what is the vision of executive leadership that we should come away with?"

"We're still analyzing that," Ken said, an answer that I first thought was either extraordinarily naïve or playfully flip. But given Ken's keen intelligence and his not to be underestimated toughness, I thought his answer was probably more of a playful but poker-faced dismissal of my grandstanding attempt to discredit the program. I was certain of this, however: Ken's answer aptly summarized the fundamental problem with the new system of executive development—it had no vision, it was not a big idea at all, and it was just another ground down analytical model. The last thing visionary executives would ever say about their strategic vision was that they were still analyzing it, because analyzing, as any visionary CEO will tell you, is in the realm of tactics not strategy. As for last things said, I decided that my comment at Ken Ivie's conference session would not be my last word on the topic of executive development, or as I preferred to call it, executive leadership. So I reorganized my notes and drafted a memo and emailed it to Eileen Boyer.

A Executives

A executives are people who within reason could have done anything they wanted to do in life.

Dear Eileen,

After hearing Ken Ivie's conference presentation on our new approach to executive leadership, I thought I'd share a few observations about what has apparently become a fait d'accompli. I'm sure you recall my comments at your advisory council meeting, the general drift of which was that the executive development program was a rather mundane approach to an idea that had some exciting possibilities. I called it banal and uninspiring, which it most certainly is, prompting me to ask—is this the best we can do? Clearly I don't think it is. I think we can do much better, but we need to think strategically about it—we are after all engaged in a strategic planning process—instead of analytically. Coming out of our first Commission meeting we had an opportunity to continue thinking strategically about the idea of A executives in our field. Rather than pursue that opportunity, we hastily turned our attention to a tactical, analytical approach. It was a little like Whitehall (the affectionate though irreverent term I often used to describe the international organization) having a dinner party and not inviting the field until dessert was done and coffee was served, at which point we were to find out what Whitehall wanted the executive program to look like. Oh yes, we could share ideas, (or I should say, details about skill sets), but the concept itself was already decided: it was to be an analytical efficiency model like the SOE's. What we needed to do was continue thinking strategically about the idea of A executives. We needed to come up with a vision of what A executives would look like before defining it in tactical terms. Instead, we looked at this whole matter like Jonathan Swift's Lilliputians looked at life, seeing it "with great exactness, but at no great distance."

The system that Whitehall wants, and it is best described as a system, has one overriding assumption: executive excellence can be brought about by defining criteria (skills and traits), then training and evaluating executives based on those criteria regardless of their talent and educational background. The system suggests that you can bootstrap a C executive up to an A, which I don't think can be done legitimately. I suppose it can be done if you fudge, if you grade-inflate like colleges and universities have done, and if most or even some of the criteria are not really related to excellence. So for me the fundamental question is: where is the talent? And once we know where the talent is, how do we attract it and retain it? And finally, do we have the talent in our field today? I don't think we do.

If you take the metaphor of a talent barrel—with a top, middle, and bottom—I think that most of our executives, ninety per cent or more, are in the middle of the barrel; and many of them are in the lower end of the middle. They are average folks, solid but undistinguished. If they were not working for us, they would be teachers, school principals, social workers, or middle managers in business. No amount of training or evaluating or defining skill sets will transform these executives into A's. They are good, solid, respectable C's. As La Rochefoucauld, the great French maximist, might have said: you cannot make a fine wine from a mediocre grape. Our problem, our strategic challenge, is not a training or systems gap; it is a talent and educational gap.

If most of our executives become executives at, say, thirty-five—it could be older or younger; it doesn't really matter—that is an age by which all, or almost all, of the top talent, the A talent, is long gone. They went to medical school, law school, graduate school. They went to work for Fortune 500 companies. They started their own businesses. They traded on Wall Street or wrote for the Wall Street Journal. But they most certainly are not in our field in any significant numbers; I would say only two to three per cent of the people in our field are A executives. I've heard you say it is ten per cent. Clyde Thompson thinks it is a much higher number. But A executives in my definition—you folks have yet to define it—are people who within reason could have done anything they wanted to do in life. They could have become a surgeon, they could have argued a case before the Supreme Court, they could have written a critically acclaimed novel, they could have become the CEO of a major corporation. They could have done any number of things. That is what I would call an A. And that is why we have precious few A executives in our field, and why we will always have a precious few if we continue down the Lilliputian path of skill development systems. But if the A executives are not knocking on our door at age 35 in any significant numbers, how can we attract them to our field before they're lost to the larger world?

The first thing we need to determine is where a significant proportion of potential A executives are. I think they're at Amherst, Swarthmore, Haverford, Barnard, Pomona and other top liberal arts colleges, and in other places as well, but predominantly at these schools, where some of the brightest and most talented young people go, where there is still a semblance of the liberal arts, and where one has some assurance that the graduates of these colleges can not only think critically and creatively but have received, through a liberal arts education, wisdom on how to live their lives. The best of these students have a great curiosity, and they came away from their college experience exemplifying the classical ideal of the life of the mind. And they came away with at least some introduction to the meaning and importance of ethics and civic engagement.

We could attract some of these young people, particularly those who have a strong sense of civic engagement, to our organization, but it would require transforming our international organization—the one thing we have that has the necessary cachet—into an engine of executive development. We could pluck these people right out of Amherst and other places and bring them to Whitehall to learn the business and get a masters degree from Harvard or some other university. We would have to pay them salaries competitive with the corporate world, and after a few years place them in the best executive positions in the field. Some could stay at Whitehall in senior management positions, but not spend their entire careers there. In fact, if the idea of an engine of executive development were extended to everyone in the international organization, not just senior executives, then presumably no one would or could make a career out of working for Whitehall. Everyone, or almost everyone, would stay five to seven years and then go back to the field to be the executive or senior manager of a local organization. But most important of all, by recruiting from the best colleges in America, we could compete directly with other fields for the best talent available, instead of hoping that these talented people serendipitously show up at our door ten to fifteen years after they leave college, instead of hoping that by some act of analytical prestidigitation we can bootstrap solid C's into more ample A's.

Finally, here's a vision, which unfortunately is lacking in the analytical model Whitehall is running with: ten years from now there will be a cover story in Parade magazine, though it could easily be the New York Times or the Wall Street Journal, in which ten thirtyish Youth Association executives are pictured on the cover—eight of whom are executives of major organizations in the field, two of whom are senior executives of the international organization. The article is about how Whitehall attracted the best young executive talent in America, and how it became the envy of not only the non-profit world but the for-profit world as well. Clearly, we never gave other executive development ideas an opportunity to percolate, we never gave thinking strategically about the topic a chance to coalesce, and I for one am left with the question I started with: Is this the best we can do? As always, my best, Michael.

When I wrote the memo to Eileen about the executive development program, I thought she would at least react to it, if not by phone, at least by email. But there was no reaction of any kind until well over a year later when we had dinner together to discuss her upcoming national conference speech. I assumed that in the interim too much time and money had been invested in the skills sets model to turn back to a more creative, strategic approach to executive development. Since Eileen had blocked most of the next morning to work on her speech, our dinner discussion turned to another topic that we periodically discussed, executive succession. This topic always started with who would succeed her and always ended with the question of who would succeed an entire generation of executives—our generation— retiring within the next decade. After going over the various candidates who could potentially succeed her—some from Whitehall, some from the field—we came to two mutually agreed upon realizations: that no one we discussed was the perfect candidate on all counts and that everyone we discussed was a member of our own generation, that generation of older baby boomers about to retire. Where were the executives in their thirties and forties who could potentially succeed Eileen?

"I can't think of anybody," I said. "But you get out in the field more than I do. There must be somebody."

"Not that I know of," Eileen said.

"Maybe we're just not attracting the right talent," I said.

"Yes, you've made that point before, pretty persuasively."

"Not persuasive enough, apparently. We're still trying to define executive leadership by cobbling together forty-nine skill sets."

I took this opening to re-explain my position on executive development. I had what amounted to a two-minute version, a five-minute version and a ten-minute version. I went with the two-minute version. With Eileen's prodigious memory, however—she actually remembered my memo almost verbatim—I could have given her the one-sentence version. I concluded by re-establishing the strategic link: "Other than your vision of generational civic engagement, this idea, the idea of the A executive, was the only other potentially big idea that came out of our strategic planning. But we let it get away. It was death by analytic overkill."

Eileen simply said, "Why couldn't we do both?" and changed the subject: "But how can we make the vision, the other big idea, as you like to call it, the centerpiece of my conference speech?" In the context of Eileen's upcoming speech, that was indeed the crucial question to ask—how to make it a vision speech—but there were other more important things on my mind regarding the powerful vision that was first forged in Eileen's opening remarks to the Commission for the 21st Century. I wondered how, for instance, we could begin to realize her vision without reducing it to the quotidian prescriptions of which her corporate bureaucracy was so fond, and how could we connect this vision to the international organization's increasingly febrile preoccupation with public trust. But the first thing we had to do was define the vision with concision, clarity, and if possible, eloquence. We knew what we wanted the vision to be, but we did not know exactly how to say it. Eileen found the language to describe our new vision in a place I would never have thought to look: a conference speech I had written for her a couple of years before. She found it the next day while we were working at the conference table in her office.

"Michael, the vision statement, here it is," she said, as she read from a printed version of a speech that she had delivered to wide acclaim in San Diego: "We envision a future in which every child can succeed, and whole generations of children are lifted to a level of civic engagement not seen since the founding of our nation." In the elevated rhetoric of an old speech, Eileen found what she had been looking for and what the Commission had been hinting at for the last year and a half: a vision more potent than anything our institution had ever contemplated, a vision so towering that its critics thought it wildly ambitious. And its ambitiousness was not limited to the grand notion that we could lift a single generation to the level of Washington and Jefferson and Hamilton and Madison, but that we could do it again and again until we had several generations of citizens engaged in making their communities better places to live, at which point we could conclude we had not only changed lives, we had changed America, one child, one community at a time. If our approach to executive development landed unceremoniously on tactical ground, our vision of the future soared to unprecedented strategic heights. Aside from my concerns about grounding our vision in petty prescriptions, I began to reflect on whether even a vision as powerful as this could compete with the new driving force of the national organization: public trust.

3

Ethics

The law constrains one to act in an appropriate way; ethics elevates one to think and act in an admirable way.

Public Relations Posing as Public Trust

The link between reputation and ethics reduces ethics to a morally dubious exercise in public relations.

During the deliberations of the Commission for the 21st Century and long after they were completed, public trust replaced growth as the predominant preoccupation of Whitehall. Growth was still important, and m&m's (money and marketing) were more important than ever, but superseding all of that was the issue of public trust. What brought about this preoccupation was not just corporate scandals like Enron and the over-reaction of the political class in Washington with poorly conceived legislation like Sarbanes-Oxley (legislation that was not applicable to non-profits anyway), but rather a major scandal within our own organization. The scandal in question, which probably would not have caught the attention of the national press if it had not occurred in New York City, involved the allegedly illegal diversion of funds from a Youth Association organization to a radio network. The details of the scandal turned out to be not as important as the fact that it was covered by the national press and, therefore, caused considerable embarrassment to the international organization. As a result of the scandal, Whitehall pressed for and got a change in our federation's constitution allowing the international organization to remove a local organization from membership without notice. Prior to the scandal, Whitehall was required to give sixty days notice before it could pull the charter of a local organization. The sixty-day provisional period had enabled an organization to fact find and to correct deficiencies that threatened the status of its charter. Now an organization's charter could be pulled without notice.

Other reforms followed, most of them proportionate to the threat potential scandals posed to the organization. As a condition of membership in the international organization, local organizations were soon required to conduct background checks on all employees, something that many organizations had already done anyway. The incident that prompted the background requirement was a local organization hiring a youth worker with a criminal record, who, while employed by the organization, committed another crime. A scandal in which another youth development organization was accused of inflating the number of kids they served led to a requirement that all local organizations have a records retention policy. When we were required to have a whistleblower policy—already a law in many states—which every employee and volunteer had to sign, it was clear to me that we were losing our sense of proportion about ethics. And with the constant drumbeat coming out of Whitehall, it was clear that our international organization was not just reacting to scandal, but overreacting to it, not just affirming an ethical position, but crusading on its behalf.

The crusade would lead to the requirement, under the banner of public trust, that every local organization have an ethics policy. Having an ethics policy was good in theory, provided that one had an accurate idea of what ethics actually was. Since our international organization, in its infinite eagerness to do good and its blind belief that it was indeed doing good, did not have a clear idea what ethics actually was, its ethical policy-making resulted in a comic irony: instead of doing the right thing for the right reasons, Whitehall's ethics policy did the wrong thing for the wrong reasons. And one of those reasons was most certainly public relations. Our regional vice-president explained Whitehall's position on ethics this way: "I know a lot of things have been coming down the pike from New York, and we all feel a little put upon because of it, but at the end of the day, these ethics policies are the right thing to do. Let's face it, folks, we have to protect our brand."

Eileen Boyer, in a speech I wrote for her, said things about ethics I would not have said myself: "Our most prized possession is our integrity, and the name Youth Association International, which is emblematic of that integrity… what we must never forget, what must remain indelible in our memory, is that our reputation took a century to build, but could be undone in a day." In another speech, which I did not write for her, she said, "It is natural for us to think that bad things cannot happen in our movement.

But they can and do happen. Over the last year alone we have seen serious incidents of financial mismanagement as well as poor judgment in hiring practices." In the same speech, she said: "Ethics, integrity, transparency and child safety must be our top priorities, not because it is the popular thing to do, but because it is the right thing to do." I'm sure that Eileen, whom I know to be a person of unimpeachable integrity, believed that her ethical position was based on doing the right thing, but the overriding reason was the protection of the institution's reputation, the protection of its brand. "Because once our brand is tarnished," as another senior executive at Whitehall put it, "our fundraising will go in the tank." Linking ethics to branding and fundraising was the first of many mistakes made by our international organization. It may be a universal business practice to protect one's brand, but it has nothing to do with ethics. Branding, which seeks to portray an organization in an almost celestial light, is inherently unethical because it gives a selectively sanguine picture of the institution. Branding is the antithesis of ethics in that it selectively ignores faults, flaws, failings. Any approach to ethics motivated by the desire to protect a brand ineluctably leads one to be less honest and less transparent. It leads to a link between reputation and ethics that reduces ethics to a morally dubious exercise in public relations.

Policies are not Prescriptions

If we were all obligated to be saints,
we would all end up as sinners.

The first requirement of any valid ethics policy is that it is conceived and executed for the right reason. Eileen Boyer had the right reason when she said that conducting ourselves in an ethical manner was the right thing to do. She need not have and gone any further than that in affirming an ethical stance. The first principle of ethics is that any inherently self-interested position cannot claim to be ethical. We could not therefore claim our stance to be ethical if its primary purpose was to protect our reputation from the vicissitudes of public scandal. Ethics has to have, as Immanuel Kant described in his **Foundations of the Metaphysics of Morals**, a pure intention. For Kant, the only thing good without exception is a good will. But the international staff at Whitehall did more than just muddle the purity of their ethical intentions; they also had the temerity to think that they could develop an ethics policy that was based on prescriptions rather than principles.

No philosopher or religious thinker in the West that I know of has been able to distill ethics into a defined set of standards or prescriptions—not Plato, not Aristotle, not Cicero, not Marcus Aurelius, not Thomas Aquinas, not Immanuel Kant, not John Stuart Mill. Perhaps the Ten Commandments, which presumably God Himself gave to Moses at Mount Sinai, comes the closest to laying down rules of ethics. These were the same Ten Commandments that the Pharisees of Jesus' time turned into a multitude of legalistic prescriptions and the same rules and Commandments that Jesus distilled down to two principles: love God and love your neighbor. But the regime at Whitehall would have none of the principled approach to ethics. They would, like the Pharisees, prescribe, and prescribe some more. They would, in full analytic overdrive, prescribe until they had eighty rules by which all employees and all volunteers were to comport themselves. They did not call the eighty statements rules; they called them principles, even though most of them were in fact regulatory rules with a legalistic tone to them, even though they reduced ethics to a legal contract, to terms of employment.

Under the sub-heading of "Conflicts of Interest," for example, Whitehall's Code of Ethics: A Matter of Trust had statements such as "I will not make any payment or provide anything of value to any public official in exchange for or because of any official act performed or to be performed (that is, provide any bribe or unlawful gratuity to anyone)." Or under a section of the Code on Assets, "Financial Reporting and Transactions:" "I will not make false or misleading entries in any books, records or reports, invoices, timesheets, expense reports or aid others in doing so." Under the heading of "Fundraising:" "I will not exaggerate a contribution by one donor to influence another donor." In the category of "Confidential and Proprietary Information:" "I will not unlawfully or improperly copy or release any material that has copyright or trademark protection." And this Orwellian touch under "Professional Conduct:" "I will be alert for and report any conduct described above or any other conduct unbecoming to the Youth Association

International by other employees."

Aside from the appalling Big Brotherism of having everyone watching everyone else, a prescription hardly in keeping with "A Matter of Trust," the implication is that the eighty prescriptions are not all there is to this gargantuan Code. There might also be other unbecoming conduct that one might observe in a colleague. And given the caveat in the Code's preamble that these so-called ethics statements do not constitute "a comprehensive list of potential concerns," one is left with the impression that more Pharisee work remains to be done.

But how much more can an institution do to expand the terms of employment? If an employee's job description and chart of work objectives amount to, say, four pages of employee obligations, how fair is it to add another six pages of ethical rules one must obey? And if a regime cannot be fair and reasonable with its employees, if it cannot operate effectively without deputizing everyone as a policing agent of the institution, can that regime and its leaders be considered ethical? Ethics without justice is not ethics at all, but rather a Machiavellian business practice in which the good is defined as getting the desired outcome—in this case, a reputation untouched by scandal.

One also is left with the impression that the statements in Whitehall's Code of Ethics do not conduce with any clarity to ethical principles, even though the preamble to the Code refers to the statements as "principles …intended as a guide in making sound judgments…" Just like Whitehall's approach to organizational effectiveness (the SOE's), just like its approach to impact (the impact model), just like its approach to executive leadership (the forty-nine skill sets), its approach to ethics was based not on principles but prescriptions, not on ideas but rules, not on a policy framework, but on a regulatory one. What Whitehall wanted to do—make its employees, and subsequently, the employees of its local organizations, ethical—was admirable but misguided. The irony was that no institution, no matter how many rules it requires one to follow, could force its employees by legal prescription to be anything but what they are: flawed human beings. A perfect reputation would require us to be perfect people; it would require us to be saints; and if we were all obligated to be saints, we would all end up as sinners.

Ethics and the Law

A true ethical stance should elevate one to think and act in an admirable way, not just in a punctiliously correct way.

While Enron and other corporate scandals caused the political class to intervene with a regulatory approach to ethics, any attempt at an historical and philosophical approach to ethics languished. We could have turned to professors and philosophers instead of lawyers and politicians to find a way out of our ethical malaise, but the reformist reaction of the political class, like earlier temperance movements in our history and the more modern anti-smoking movement, was too self-righteous to be persuaded otherwise. One of the other miscalculations was to think, as Cicero did, that ethics would always inform, and in a sense, replace, politics. This is as mistaken as Machiavelli's view that politics would replace ethics. The regulatory approach of Sarbanes-Oxley turns out not to be ethics at all. Though it has moral intent, it is strictly a legal approach. The law does little more than constrain one to act in an appropriate way. Ethics has a more noble and ambitious intention. Ethics attempts to elevate one to think and act in an admirable way.

My own organization eschewed the regulatory rules approach to ethics in favor of a principled approach rooted in western philosophy. My board discussed and approved an ethics policy that was a mere eighty-three words long: "The purpose of the ethics policy of the Youth Association of Erie is to create a climate in which good judgment is guided by truthfulness, fairness and respect for the rights of others; that any decisions made or actions taken not serve any self interest, but rather be good actions for the right reasons to benefit the children served; and that this climate encourage all who act on its behalf—board, staff and volunteers—to aspire to what is admirable in their pursuits."

It may not be readily apparent that the above ethics policy had its origins in western philosophy, in ideas as old as the ancient Greeks, but it does. It actually touches upon three pure theories of ethics: the theory of the right, which one can find in Plato but perhaps gets its most famous expression in Kant's idea of a good will; the theory of the good, which one can also find in Plato and Aristotle but also a more modern expression in the utilitarianism of Jeremy Bentham and John Stuart Mill; and the theory of the good life, a life not only prized but praised, a life not only enviable but admirable, which found its best expression in Plato's **Philebus** and Aristotle's **The Nicomachean Ethics**.

What, then, does my organization's ethics policy mean in practical as opposed to theoretical terms? In practical terms our principled approach to ethics means that anything we do or say has to have a pure intention. Simply put, it means that we have to say what we say and do what we do for the right reasons. We cannot refrain from making "false or misleading entries in any books" to protect our reputation or our brand, which is self-serving, and therefore not ethical. Instead, we have to refrain from engaging in financial malfeasance because it violates the ethical principle of truthfulness. And when the principle of truthfulness becomes an integral part of our ethical practice, we find ourselves elevated to that which is admirable instead of constrained by that which is legally expedient and publicly self-serving. But even the purest intentions can have negative consequences, which is why we must also consider the ethical outcomes of our actions and decisions.

Our policy refers to "good actions for the right reasons." What are good actions? For utilitarians like Bentham and Mill, a good action means doing the greatest good for the greatest number. The problem with the utilitarian approach to ethics is that the greatest good might actually be bad for the few in the minority. Whitehall's requirement that all employees sign a pledge to obey the Code of Ethics for Employees may indeed constrain more employees to be more ethical in more situations, but what if a few employees, or even one employee, believe that its self-policing provision is an unfair—even illegal—employment practice? Certainly an ethics code that is not fair or abridges the rights of employees is really not ethical, which is why getting an ethical outcome requires our actions and our decisions to be tempered by justice and by a concern for individual rights.

Our ethics policy, as opposed to Whitehall's, has as its goal to do the good thing for the right reason. The way to accomplish that goal is to be guided by truthfulness, fairness and respect the rights of others. As a youth development agency, the way for us to accomplish our ethical goal is to act not in self interest but in the best interest of the children we serve. But doing the good thing for the right reason, which is not always easy to do, is not enough to satisfy the transcendent nature of a truly ethical stance. A true ethical stance should elevate one to think and act in an admirable way, not just a punctiliously correct way.

Permanent Concerns

Each generation has to discover itself in
relation to the permanent concerns of mankind.
~Allan Bloom

So what does it mean to think and act in an admirable way? Plato's view was that "to know the good is to do the good." But even in this age of ethical re-awakening prompted by corporate scandal, most people I encounter have neither read about nor reflected on the topic of ethics, certainly not from the classical perspective of Plato and Aristotle, not even from the more contemporary perspective of writers like W.D. Ross and Alasdair MacIntyre. As a result, many of them have almost no ethical content, the exception perhaps being those for whom the practice of religion is a serious and thoughtful expression of a higher life. But absent living a higher life informed by religious faith, where does one turn for the wisdom to live an ethical life, a good life? Where does one turn to examine the permanent questions inherent in living a good life?

With the near demise of liberal arts education, we are no longer educated to consider the permanent or universal questions, though the nature of the good life is one of those permanent questions that every generation ought to consider. I do not believe that even the brightest and best educated people of my generation—I am at the older end of the baby boomer generation—have given more than passing consideration to what really constitutes the good life. Yet it is precisely these kinds of questions that define a generation. For Allan Bloom "each generation has to discover itself in relation to the permanent concerns of mankind." But to follow Bloom's argument one first has to accept that there are permanent questions to consider and that it is worth the effort to read and reflect on what the greatest minds had to say about these questions. Bloom, who was of an earlier generation, believed great books could convey the wisdom of the ages, wisdom that would be of great value to us in the here and now. My generation, with the exception of a few classicists and philosophers in academia, does not believe that great books can convey the wisdom we need to live our lives admirably, ethically, successfully. For the younger generations, particularly the one occupying our colleges and universities in the first decade of the 21st century, the idea that they ought to ponder the permanent questions first raised by the ancients is so remote as to be utterly quaint and irrelevant. This is the generation that will complete the transformation of higher education into an exercise in career preparation and economic opportunism.

A recent conversation I had with one of my youngest daughter's university classmates is illustrative of higher education's accommodation to careerism. When I asked this young man what he was studying at the university, he said, "Chemistry."

"Why chemistry?" I asked.

"I want to be a dentist," he said.

"What kind of dentist?"

"Cosmetic dentistry," he said. "Veneers."

I found this young man to be very bright. He had thoughtful opinions on public issues, but like the rest of his generation he will not get the opportunity to consider Bloom's permanent questions in any systematic or thoughtful way. He will study hard, get straight A's, go to dental school, practice dentistry, and live if not the good life at least an enviable one full of financial success. Not every college kid has a career outlook as concentrated as this young man, but it does point out how narrow and self-interested our current approach to higher education can be. Where will this young man's philosophy of ethics come from? A pastor possibly? From moral lessons taught by his parents? From a philosophy class taken to fulfill a humanities requirement? Probably not from a sustained and systematic effort to think about ethical questions while still a student at the university. What would lead him to think about the mixed life that Aristotle described in **The Nicomachean Ethics**, one that is both prized (self-interested) and praised (directed outward from the self)? This young man will probably find what is prized in life: a good job, a nice car, a beautiful home, opportunities for travel. All of these things bring one pleasure in the utilitarian sense, but they only constitute a part of the good life. If one's life concentrated only on what is prized, it would be by definition self-centered. If one's life concentrated, as Gandhi's did, only on a self-sacrificial quest for justice, it too would lack the ideal mean of Aristotle's good life. The mean that represents Aristotle's good life is not an average life but a life that achieves a point of excellence between the extremes of total self-interest and total self-sacrifice. For a life to be worthy of praise it must have something at its core that transcends the self, but it need not be strictly self-sacrificial. The theoretical life, the life of the mind, transcends the practical considerations of self by seeking the wisdom of a larger truth. It is what Socrates called the examined life, and for Socrates the unexamined life was not worth living.

The Good Life

Much of our ethical confusion comes from the fact that we cannot place our professional life in the classical context of a good life.

For the modern philosopher Robert Nozick, "the unexamined life is not lived as fully." Nozick believes that the self can be transformed by love, friendship, and religious quest. He plots this idea graphically by drawing a circle within a circle. In a love relationship the boundaries of the self expand from one circle to two: a smaller circle within a larger circle. One circle is the "I" and one circle is the "we." If the smaller circle within the larger circle is the "I," then that individual is concerned more with other than with self. If the smaller circle within the larger circle is the "we," then that individual is more concerned with self than with other.

In a good life, would the "I" and the "we" be in perfect equilibrium, or would one or the other predominate and constitute the core of one's being or soul? Would there be a constant tension between the "I" and "we" of one's soul? And if there were such a tension, what part of the soul would be more likely to encroach on the other part? Would the inner circle of the soul be stronger as if it constituted a core, or would the outer circle be stronger because it enveloped the smaller inner circle? Nozick does not address the question of whether there is a tension or an equilibrium in what I have chosen to define as bipolar parts of the soul, but he does suggest that the larger outer circle is predominant. I personally have never met anyone I would characterize as purely a "we" with no inner "I." I suppose that such a description might fit Gandhi or Jesus or Buddha, maybe Martin Luther King in our own time. But I have met many people whom I would describe as purely an "I," and there is not much admirable about them. Their souls are devoid of anything beyond self. What our ethics ought to concern itself with—other than pure intentions and good outcomes—is nurturing an equilibrium in the souls of our citizens, an equilibrium in which the "we" is as large and as potent as the "I." But how does one take a philosophical abstraction like this and make it relevant to our own lives and to our professional lives?

Nozick argues, as did Plato before him, that we have to be concerned about the whole of our being, that for Plato, the harmonious life, the good life, can only be arrived at by having the rational part of the soul ruling the other two parts: the courageous and the passionate. What I would argue is that, to create an equilibrium in the souls of our citizens, the admirable part of our souls (that which is praised) should not so much rule over the enviable (that which is prized) as to be strong enough to reign in the passions of self interest. This would encourage our citizens to live more admirable, virtuous lives. It would encourage them to live more ethical lives.

But to do so, the critical question we should

ask, in fact the ethical question every generation should ask itself, is not what we should do in any particular situation in accordance with some particular rule or prescription. That kind of approach to ethics, according to Alasdair MacIntyre, leads to moral and ethical incoherence. The critical question for Aristotle and for all of ancient and medieval ethics was not what to do in particular situations, but who we ought to be. The emphasis is not on our actions, although ultimately our actions come into play, but on our values, on our principles, on what the ancients would call our virtues. So the critical question to ask is not what should we do, but rather who should we be.

I'm arguing that we should be people who tell the truth, are fair and just, and respect the rights of others. I'm arguing that we should be people in whom self interest is tempered by a deep commitment to the admirable things in life. But how does one apply this notion of ethics, of the good life, to one's life as a non-profit executive? One cannot find the answer to this question in any contemporary business book on the shelf of the local book store, though one might find it in the public library. Nor can one find the wisdom to live one's professional life in any legislation coming out of Washington. The answer lies not in the platitudes and prescriptions of business books, nor in the legalistic pontifications of Congress, but rather in seeing the professional as part of a whole life lived well—a good life.

Separating the personal from the professional, a practice now common in our national politics, leads to a dichotomy in the soul, turning one into an ethically disjointed Jekyll and Hyde. This is the double life to which we have accommodated ourselves in modernity, not the good life that the classical world still affords us. Much of our ethical confusion comes from the fact that we cannot place our professional life in the classical context of a good life. If one were to plot the professional part of one's life with Nozick's concentric circles, the larger circle would be the life lived well, the good life, and the smaller circle within would be the professional life. For so many of us the ethical connection between the two spheres, the personal and the professional, is tenuous, and in some, completely bifurcated into two separate spheres.

But if ethics comes down to who we are rather than the sum of our organizations rules and regulations, then organizations themselves are not ethical entities and cannot claim to be intrinsically ethical based upon ethics policy prescriptions. These prescriptions are little more than ethical ornament. Not that the ethical prescriptions of institutions like Whitehall are intended to deceive. Whitehall's ethical prescriptions are intended to protect the reputation of the institution. They are intended to protect the brand. They are intended to secure, and forever maintain, the public's trust.

The real deception is that these prescriptions cannot possibly achieve these intentions, at least not without employees (better yet: think of them in the broader human context as people) who already see themselves as truth-tellers and the like. The prescriptive approach ultimately leads an institution to deceive itself into believing it stands on high moral ground, when in fact it has fallen into a valley of analytical incoherence. Nonprofit institutions will not be able to rise above this ethical incoherence unless they ask the right questions: it is not what kind of employees are working for them, but rather what kind of people are working for them; it is not what their people ought to do in any given situation, but rather who their people ought to be.

But bringing the personal and the professional spheres together will undoubtedly be extraordinarily difficult for most nonprofits. In the case of the Youth Association International, our vision provides us with the perfect opportunity to ground our ethical philosophy in a classical conception of the good life.

Consider our vision: to lift whole generations of young people to a level of civic engagement not seen since the founding of our nation. That is a towering vision of the future. It is a vision of a higher life, a good life, an admirable life. It is a vision capable of solving our ethical conundrum—if, that is, it can be applied not only to the kids we serve, but also to the professionals men and women who serve them. Then the professionals too can be lifted to a level of civic engagement not seen since the founding of our nation. They too can be inspired to live an admirable life, an ethical life, a life in which their souls as citizens find an equilibrium between what is admirable (other directed by civic engagement) and enviable (self directed by the pursuit of pleasure), a life in which the admirable in them is expansive enough to circumscribe the enviable. Then they too can live the good life.

Messina

4

Prelude

There are two methods of curing
the mischiefs of faction:
the one, by removing the causes;
the other by controlling its effects.
~James Madison

A Board Divided

An ideal board is a collection of individuals with no
factional connections to each other
and whose collective will is only expressed
in their support of the mission, vision,
and core principles of the institution.

Can a vision of the future, however admirable it may be, solve an ethical conundrum that is timeless and universal? Can a vision of the future bring one's soul into perfect equilibrium when one is constantly confronted with the Machiavellians of the world, with intriguers who could, through superior political cunning, bring one, as Machiavelli's put it, to grief. Tommy Di-

Tullio, though he had no personal wealth—he lived in a modest house, drove a modest car and lived on a modest government pension—was my most potent board member, which made him in true Palmerstonian fashion my most important ally early in our relationship and my most formidable enemy later in our relationship. What made him so potent is that he knew everyone in town, from high to low to everyone in between, and he not only knew everyone on the board, he knew most of their spouses because he had personally delivered to their homes prosciutto and homemade wine at Christmas and candy and cake at Easter. Sometimes he would even throw in a picture of one of the saints which he would then say was personally blessed by the Pope. But other than having too much access to me and too much influence on who came on to the board and who went off, Tommy was dangerous in two other important respects.

First, like Iago, Tommy harbored a deep grudge, not against a man, an Othello, but against a class, the WASPS—the wealthy, the well-born, the financially successful businessmen like Peter Matthews, about whom nothing, not his car, not his house, not his personality, was modest. As the twelfth of thirteen children of Italian immigrants, Tommy carried with him feelings of inferiority that pulled his soul into a single circle of self interest. It was almost daily that he railed against some WASP like Matthews. And if Tommy was perceptive enough to point out the pride of a Matthew Mihalak, he was oblivious to its manifestation in himself. He did not see the pride he took in politically outmaneuvering a class of people he disdained. Second, Tommy did not see that he had an insatiable need for recognition. I did not see it in him either until it was too late, years after I met him and saw in Tommy's house all of his accolades—plaques, trophies, ribbons, proclamations. Apparently every organization he had ever joined, and he joined them all, had honored him, mostly at his own instigation. People with feelings of inferiority are not inherently dangerous. Nor are people who are needy for recognition. But those rare souls whose ambition is burning for recognition and whose pride is punctured by feelings of inferiority are decidedly dangerous.

Given Tommy's tirades against the WASPS, had I seen all of his accolades earlier on, I might have listened to Peter Matthews's advice, which was to tell Tommy to stay away, but not before I let Tommy drive Matthews and his faction from the board. For once a board is divided into factions, it is an act of political carelessness to allow one faction to prevail over another. Better that both factions fail, and the board is rebuilt from the bottom up. An ideal board is a collection of individuals with no factional connections to each other, whose collective will is expressed only in their support of the mission, vision and core principles of the institution. The presence of factions on the board of directors is a sign that an institution is in distress, and that it must be wholly rebuilt by turning over almost all of its membership in the shortest time possible: a year or two if possible, three or four if necessary.

Factions form in various ways. Allowing one influential board volunteer to do virtually all of the board recruitment, as was the case with Tommy DiTullio, is one way that a board becomes factionalized. A way for CEOs to counter this state of affairs is to do the recruiting themselves, carefully avoiding the recruitment of volunteers with close social or professional ties to current members of the board. Another way is to keep the committee structure as fluid as possible. Have few standing committees, and rotate the membership of these committees from time to time. Have much of the board's work done by ad hoc committees or task groups which meet to accomplish a specific task and then are disbanded. By making the committee structure of the institution fluid, factions are discouraged.

Unfortunately, I did none of these things, while factional forces, particularly those loyal to Tommy, started to line up against me. Instead, I wavered while Tommy waged war on the WASPS, and I never followed up by waging my own war on him and his friends. Instead, I stood by while Tommy consolidated his control over the organization, and I never sought any alliances of my own. Roughly half of the remaining board volunteers would have been open, quietly, anonymously, one-by-one, to an alliance with me to limit Tommy's authority in the organization. But I would have had to schedule these meetings on my own. By this time Meg Michalsky, who was once Tommy's enemy but was now his friend, was communicating my every move to Tommy. The purpose of my one-on-one meetings with these relatively neutral board members would have been to elicit their concerns, rather than expressing my concerns about Tommy.

This tactic, coupled with a careful screening of and a more active role in recruiting volunteers to replace those who left the organization, would probably have given me the majority I needed to drive Tommy out of the organization.

Tommy still controlled the nominating committee, but I believed my current president, Curt Schroeder, would have been amenable to reorganizing the committees, even to the point of replacing Tommy as nominating committee chair. Curt Schroeder was an old guard member of the board with some loyalty to the Matthews and Robertson crowd. This became more apparent to me at an annual meeting when, after listening to a wine-woozy Tommy barely get through his nominating report, I overheard Curt Schroeder say, with a sigh of exasperation, "Well, we got through another one." This should have been my opening, given that we were beginning the last year of Curt Schroeder's two-year term as president, to persuade Curt to re-organize the committees and replace Tommy as nominating chair. Tommy, always overly sensitive to any slight, might have quit the board in a huff, and might have taken his old City Hall colleague, Maria DiSanto, with him. But I did not act, and a year later Curt Schroeder formed a friendship with his old enemy Tommy DiTullio, but not before the tumultuous presidency of Larry Miller had begun.

Rising to the Presidency

It is critically important
that the right people rise to the presidency,
and the wrong people do not. It is equally important
that they rise for the right reasons.

Larry Miller was a big folksy southerner who came to town many years ago to play basketball for one of the local universities. His athletic career as back-up center on the university basketball team and his professional career as a mid manager of one of the utility companies were respectable but undistinguished. As an athlete he came off the bench for most of his career, and as a manager he was a back-bencher who never got close to the highest levels of management. But he was a big and amiable guy who seemed genuinely interested in making an impact on the community.

Larry had been recruited for the board by Tommy DiTullio a few years before I came to the organization, and over time distinguished himself as a fundraiser. Early in my tenure Larry agreed, at my urging as much as Tommy's, to chair our annual drive, which he did very successfully for three consecutive years. In appreciation of his fundraising efforts, I asked Larry to present our most prestigious award at our annual fundraising dinner. Larry seemed surprised and honored that I asked him, too honored, as I reflect on it now. He presented the award in front of a crowd of four hundred people, which he did awkwardly but charmingly. The presentation had the salutary effect of instantaneously raising his stature in the community. It was one of those rare moments when a previously little known actor memorably arrives on the community stage. Larry Miller, a small-town guy from Dothan, Alabama, who had ventured north thirty-five years ago to make his way in the world, had suddenly arrived. And I had not so suddenly orchestrated it.

But there was still more orchestrating to be done for Larry Miller. I advocated for, and got, an expedited route for Larry to the presidency of the organization. Instead of going through two intermediate chairs, treasurer and vice-president,

I suggested to Tommy's nominating committee, with Tommy's endorsement, that Larry be elevated from secretary of the board to president-elect. Two years later Larry Miller was the first African American to become president of the Board of Directors of our local Youth Association. And even though I had known Larry for several years now, I would soon find out who the real Larry Miller was and what his real intentions were. So it is worth pondering how Larry got into the position of power in the organization. I say **the** position of power because, next to a strong CEO, the board president, by virtue of his power of appointment, is the most powerful position in any non-profit organization, which makes it critically important that the right people rise to the presidency, and the wrong people, the Larry Miller's and Tommy DiTullio's, do not. It is equally important that they rise for the right reasons. Larry Miller's rise was for all the wrong reasons.

All non-profits are pre-occupied with fundraising; some, like the Youth Association International, are passionately pre-occupied to the point of fixation. Even with a more moderate concentration on raising money, our organization still established fundraising proficiency as the key criterion in the selection of our board presidents. Larry Miller's success as a fundraiser was perhaps the primary reason I advocated for his rise to the presidency of the organization. It was a test that we applied to all incoming volunteers, almost all of whom began as a trustee: a volunteer who had a vote only at the annual meeting and could serve only on fundraising committees rather than standing or ad hoc committees. To get elected to the board of directors, a trustee would have to demonstrate, among other things, proficiency as a fundraiser. And as long as the "other things" remained of paramount importance—checking the backgrounds of prospective board volunteers and recruiting people not needy for recognition or motivated by self-aggrandizement—a fundraising test could be applied to new volunteers coming into the organization. But not to potential presidents. Good fundraisers do not necessarily make good leaders, and electing presidents almost exclusively on that basis invariably puts the real fundamentals at risk: mission, vision, and ethics. Larry Miller, like his mentor Tommy DiTullio, compromised all three to satisfy the twin passions of self-interest and public recognition.

Proportionalism and Identity Politics

While I had been able to win an engagement on a bigger battlefield with the proportionalists and their passion for identity politics, I would not be so lucky on a smaller one.

Race was the other reason for Larry Miller's rise to the presidency of the organization. Though the clientele we served had changed since our founding in 1895, when it was the sons of Russian, Italian and Polish immigrants, to the 1960s when it was still all boy and almost all white and largely poor or working class, to the present day membership of boys and girls (boys by a small majority), mostly black (sixty-five per cent) and very poor (eighty per cent living at or below the poverty line), the governance of the institution had not changed much at all. There were a few women now and two African Americans, including Larry Miller, whereas the remainder of the board looked like the old literary canon: all white guys, a few in their thirties and forties, but most of them over fifty, and two in their eighties. I cannot say this with absolute certainty, but to a man the canonical crowd all seemed to feel a palpable sense of pride in the fact that, in an age when the idea of diversity was spoken of in reverential tones, our organization was the only largely white agency in town to elect a black president. I could hear in the sidebar comments, I could see in the body language and facial expressions, that we were all quite proud of ourselves, of our racial magnanimity and our high-minded embrace of diversity.

There was at least one leader in the black community who made it known that he was unimpressed with our liberal largesse. His argument was that, to achieve a true sense of diversity, our board and staff would need a composition that reflected the demographics of our membership. Since the majority of the kids we served were black, his logic predicated that a majority of our board and staff should be black. As it stood, only twenty per cent of our staff was black and only five per cent of the board. The problems in a race-based system of this kind are plainly obvious. For agencies like the Scouts and the YMCA, who serve very few minorities, it would mean that only whites could serve on their boards and work for their agencies. And if one extended this race-based approach to gender, it would require half the board and staff to be female. But the real speciousness of this position lies in the attempt to draw a direct connection between kids who are members and the adult talent pool from which an organization could reasonably build a staff and a board of directors. Since the kids themselves are not the talent pool, then one must turn to the real talent pool to see who is actually available to serve and to work. With a county population only five per cent black, trying to build a board and staff from such a small pool of talent would make mediocrity, perhaps even institutional decline, difficult to avoid—all for the privilege of being captive to the identity politics.

I heard another version of this proportionalist argument at a national task force meeting I attended. This time the argument was made by the feminists at the table. Their argument was that not only should the membership of every Youth Association clubhouse be made up of boys and girls in equal proportion, but every program offered should prescribe that half the participants be female. I listened to the debate for a while as a coalition formed between white female feminists and liberal black males. One proportionalist fact was incontrovertible: roughly half of the youth population of America was male, half female, but Youth Association clubhouses, which were all-boy organizations until they began to change in the sixties, had stubbornly remained, nationally at least, about sixty per cent male and forty per cent female. I decided not to challenge the feminists who were quite passionate about their proportionalist position, but instead challenged the liberal male contingent, particularly one very bright young guy who was so fond of his own voice that he had found it necessary to comment on virtually everything everybody else said.

When I finally got the floor, I turned to this young man and said, "Quentin, since you are probably going to comment on my comment, I thought I would save you the trouble and direct this question to you. Since you are so enamored with this proportionalist idea, why just apply it to gender? Why not also to race?"

"I don't see how that's relevant to our conversation," he said.

I thought Quentin was either flummoxed or he was stalling to regroup and counterattack. So I continued: "Why shouldn't an issue as important as race be considered on proportionalist grounds too?"

Still no comment from Quentin.

I went on. "What is the black population of the U.S.?"

"Twelve per cent," he said. "So?"

"So if we applied the same draconian rule to race as has been applied to gender, then does that mean we only allow twelve per cent of our Agency memberships to be black, and the rest would be, what, mostly white?"

Outflanked, the feminists lost their black male allies and the measure lost its majority support. I had been able to win an engagement on a bigger battlefield with the proportionalists and their passion for identity politics, but I would not be so lucky on a smaller one.

Makers of Kings and Queens

CEOs are the makers of kings and queens
in their own little realms.
The king I created was full of sound and fury,
but he ultimately signified nothing but naked hubris.

In the first stages of the fight to come, I would not be so lucky with Larry Miller. Battles would be lost, but could the war with Larry Miller and Tommy DiTullio over who would control the organization ultimately be won? Even the prelude to this war, a war that my mentor Patrick McSweeney would call the palace coup, revealed lessons about the politics of nonprofits that I will carry with me the rest of my career. The first warning I recognized was the tremendous influence a CEO exercises in promoting board members to positions of leadership, especially the most important leadership position (other than that of nominating chair), the president of the organization. Larry Miller simply would not have become president if I had not promoted his candidacy at every turn. As nonprofit CEOs we empower board volunteers. We give them or advocate giving them assignments that raise their visibility and their stature. We ask them to do things that broaden their experience as board volunteers and community leaders, and we convince others to elevate them to positions of authority in the institution. CEOs, the good ones at least, the ones who seize power not for themselves and who exercise that power wisely, are the makers of kings and queens in their own little realms. The king I had created was full of sound and fury, and he ultimately signified nothing but naked hubris.

But kings and queens are also created by institutional inertia, with the idea of succession being its most typical manifestation. In one sense we did not punctiliously follow the line of succession. Larry Miller was vaulted into the presidency without having served as treasurer and vice president. Most succession plans at least prescribe a term as treasure before becoming president. But this would only have delayed the inevitable with Larry. A larger problem surrounding the selection of presidents is the sense of inevitability that is created for virtually everybody who becomes an officer. No system of succession is perfect, but it is better that no officer position automatically lead to the presidency, even president-elect.

In an age of political correctness, gender and race can also become powerful levers of inevitability. Larry Miller's lever was race. Perhaps, as Shelby Steele has observed, we were looking for absolution in Larry's expedited rise to the presidency of the organization. Perhaps we were looking for atonement, for a way to assuage our sense of guilt about the injustices of race. But this is exactly how political correctness conduces to bad judgment, how one injustice perversely creates another. In theory a board can be all white or all black. It can be all male or all female. It can be any combination of gender, race, age, ethnicity, knowledge, education and background—as long as each individual board volunteer can contribute something significant to the institution, and can contribute it independent of any factional identity. Independence and impact are all important in the role board volunteers play and in the value they add to the institution.

The cold hard reality is that we did an injustice to Larry Miller and to ourselves by promoting his rise to the presidency. What we should have done was remain race and gender neutral. We should have been practitioners of the exemplary ethic of fairness. We should have picked a person to lead who had a command of leadership's most important qualities: a sense of fairness and a sense of proportion. Larry Miller lacked both. This is not to say that nonprofits should look for leaders who are safe, moderate, mediocre. Nonprofits should look for leaders who are self-assured rather than needy for recognition, who are interested in the strategic rather than the tactical, who concentrate on the vision of the institution rather than its program execution. They should look for leaders who can conceive of something big themselves or at least have their attention commanded by the big idea of someone else. They should look for hedgehogs, not foxes. Larry Miller was, in the broadest meaning of the term, a fox. He was likeable and clever, but petty, small-minded, and wholly self-interested—as was his chief ally and sponsor on the board, Tommy DiTullio.

Small Things

While I was bold about big things,
I was careless about little things.

Although Tommy continued to come to the office after Larry's election as president, the invitations to go with him to community events and political gatherings were less frequent now. He took Larry, his new protégé, to most of these events. Sometimes Tommy would recruit a crew to go to a community event, and he would ask me to drive everybody in one of the organization's vans. The crew usually included Larry Miller, Maria DiSanto, and two others members of the board Tommy had recruited in recent years: Larry's old college coach, Ed Bolden, and Connie Santone, a young public relations executive with a political consulting background.

The first time we did this as a group, Tommy said to me the moment we arrived, "Why don't you go to the bar and get us some drinks."

"You want a red wine?" I said.

"Yeah, get everybody a drink," he said.

I knew Tommy well enough to know that, like his mentor the late mayor, he prided himself in never having to pay for anything. "Why don't I get you a wine; they can take care of themselves."

Tommy's eyes always roved around his surroundings, but now they seemed to fix themselves high and away, giving him a glassy look. "You can take care of that."

"You mean have the organization pay for it?"

Tommy winced at my lack of subtlety, at my unwillingness to do what he wanted without his having to say it explicitly. "Out of petty cash," he said in a hushed tone.

"I would need a receipt," I said, "which I could not possibly get at that bar." It was a temporary cash-only bar in the ballroom of a social club.

"Never mind," Tommy said as he abruptly turned away and headed for the bar and ordered himself a glass of wine.

A few minutes later Larry Miller said to me, in that sonorous southern drawl of his, "Hey Michael, you gonna buy me a Budweiser?"

"Sure, Larry," I said, saying to myself, "Like Tommy, like Larry."

On another occasion we all went to lunch together. I drove everybody in an agency van that I would take home with me if it was an evening event we were attending. Since this was a luncheon, we met at my office and drove to the restaurant from there. It was Tommy's favorite restaurant, an Italian landmark located in the heart of Little Italy. Tommy had a special corner table that was his any time he wanted it. Because it was two days before Christmas, Tommy was assured of having all his favorite foods: baccala, tripe and polenta. All the members of Tommy's inner circle, except Bobby Hathaway, were there: Larry Miller, Maria DiSanto, Ed Bolden and Connie Santone. After too much food and drink and plenty of holiday laughter and conviviality, I suddenly realized, as our waitress brought the bill, that I was not along just to drive: I was there to pay the bill, which the waitress handed to me after Tommy nodded in my direction and said, "Give it to my brother." Tommy's use of the word "brother" was a reminder to me that we were not as close as we once were. For some inexplicable reason, I was no longer Tommy's boy, his brother, his protégé. I was more like a cousin once removed. It appeared that Larry was now playing tyro to Tommy's tutor, but as I later learned, Larry was going it alone. Larry, though he badly needed the counsel of someone wiser than he, would ultimately rely on the faulty counsel of one: himself.

My laughter as the waitress handed me the check was intended to be outwardly good-natured, but I sensed some irony must have shown through. "So this is my treat," I said.

"Yeah, your treat," Tommy said, straight-faced as the others laughed.

"It's a Christmas tradition," one of them said above the laughter.

"The director buys," said another to more laughter.

As I studied the bill, Tommy said, "Give that bill to Ed."

Ed said, "Give it to Tommy."

"Just put it on your expense report," Tommy said.

I looked around the table, and starting with Ed Bolden there were nods of acceptance all around. But rather than pay the bill myself, which is what I should have done, I put it on my credit card and billed it to my expense account. I did not know it then, but ethical lapses like these were noticed, by Tommy who encouraged them and Meg Michalsky who booked them. Billing a non-business luncheon to my expense account and using an organization vehicle to facilitate it seemed small and unimportant to a big picture person like me. As a leader who believed in being bold, who believed that no vision was too towering, too ambitious, I believed then, and still do, that bureaucratic tendencies are a bane to nonprofits, and that those who insist on knowing the measure of everything ultimately know the value of nothing. But any idea, however good it is, can be extended too far. My aversion to the quotidian was one of those overextended ideas. While I was bold about big things, I was careless about little things like expense reports and vehicle use, things that did indeed matter. I should have known that these ethical errors could and would be used against me. What I could not have known is that there would be other more serious things that were completely conjured up and ascribed to me.

Mischief-Maker

And with one roguish remark, a mischief-maker conjured up an allegation for the coup to come.

Not long after the Christmas luncheon, Tommy showed up at the office late one morning after working out at the Y—his perennial cup of coffee in hand—and promptly paged Ryan Doyle to report to my office. Ryan was my director of operations. He had replaced the ax-wielding Evelyn Wagner, who had left the organization on her own not-so-amicable terms. Ryan was one of several staff members whose company Tommy particularly enjoyed. The staff was equally taken with Tommy, who had a nickname for every one of them, except Ryan Doyle. Ryan, a big bear of a man, was simply Doyle. I did not have to ask why Tommy had paged Ryan. It was typical of Tommy to call staff to the office. He enjoyed their company, and they enjoyed his. If there was not anyone around for Tommy to engage, he would seek somebody out, as he had sought out Ryan on this particular day.

"Doyle," Tommy said when he saw Ryan standing in the doorway of my office.

Tommy was sitting regally in his usual place: on the brown vinyl sofa along the wall perpendicular to my desk. I was seated at my desk with Tommy to my right. The rest of my office was taken up with a large conference table that could comfortably seat ten people.

"C'mon in, Doyle," Tommy said, waving a hand in the direction of the conference table. "Let's dialogue."

Ryan walked in, turned one of the conference chairs to face us, and sat down.

"Doyle, you're a mystery man," Tommy said. "I come here the other day and you're nowhere to be found."

Ryan was silent for a moment as if trying to remember where he had been. "I was at a meeting," he said finally.

"Don't con me, Doyle. That was Howard Sinden's old line when he'd get lost and no one knew where he was. But don't worry, Doyle. I'm going to respect that. You know why I'm going to respect that? Because you always respect a dog for its master. Never forget that, Doyle.

That's one of the most important lessons you will ever learn."

But Ryan was still trying to remember where he was the day that Tommy could not find him. "Maybe that's the day I was painting the pool," Ryan said.

"You don't paint a pool," Tommy said.

"The walls, Tommy, not the pool."

"Let your maintenance guy do that," Tommy said. "You shouldn't be doing that."

"Our maintenance guy was doing it. We were just helping him."

"Don't remind me," I said. "I've got some painting to do at my house."

Tommy took a last swig of coffee and poured what was left in his Styrofoam cup into the plant next to the sofa. "You shouldn't have to do that painting, either," he said to me.

I laughed. "I didn't," I said, completely missing Tommy's point.

"At your house, I mean."

"Yeah, right," I said, still not catching Tommy's connotation.

"For a smart guy, you're stunat sometimes, Palermo. Do you think when the mayor had some painting to do at his house he did it himself or hired some contractor to do it? A crew would be sent up there to take care of it."

"Of city employees?" I said, naively, incredulously.

Tommy's laughter had a sly, slow, devilish tone to it. "Why sure," he said.

"I'm not the mayor," I said.

"You don't have to be," Tommy said. Now it was he who had missed my meaning.

"All that needs to be done," Tommy continued, "is for Doyle here to pull a crew together and take care of it for you."

And with one roguish remark, a mischief-maker conjured up an allegation for the coup to come.

Eeny, meeny, miney, moe

Our acquiescence on the issue of race would become a wound we could not heal.

Just then Meg Michalsky walked into my office through the open doorway. She said hello to Tommy but ignored Ryan. She placed on my desk a small stack of mail she had opened and stamped with the day's date, and a copy of the monthly financial statements for my review.

As Meg turned to go, Tommy asked how her family was.

"Everybody's fine, Tommy."

"Your kids?'

"Fine."

"Your boyfriend?"

Meg was an attractive woman but with a dour disposition, made even more disagreeable when her mouth tightened to a thin line of displeasure. "He's doing okay," she said.

I knew, as did Tommy and Ryan, that things were not okay at home. I knew that because over time I had become a surrogate big brother who patiently listened to Meg's melancholic complaints.

"Any time you need anything, you just let me know," Tommy said.

"Sure Tommy," Meg said as she walked out of my office with a dubious huff of laughter.

When Meg was gone, Tommy said, "That boyfriend of hers. This is a guy who got mugged by some tizzuns. Then she brings this guy into her house. Now he's around her kids. That's not right. I have no respect for her. I tried to set her up with a nice guy. She goes for this guy? No, you can't respect that. No way."

"Who did you try to fix her up with, Tommy?" I said. "A nice guy like you?"

Tommy looked to Ryan. "See how he gets with me. See how he breaks 'em for me."

Ryan, who disliked Meg as much as she disliked him, pressed Tommy for an answer. "Who did you try to fix her up with, Tommy?"

"Ed Bolden likes her," Tommy said with his sly, slow laugh.

"He's almost twice her age," I said. "And he's on the board, Tommy."

Tommy had slouched down on the sofa, his head resting against the top contour of the cushion. "Ed would be perfect for her."

"He's on the board," I repeated.

"Ed's got the right stuff to take care of Meg's problem," Tommy said as he gave a quick jab with his fist.

"Yeah," Ryan said, laughing, offering a jab of his own. "But maybe Larry Miller beat Ed to the punch. He and Meg were seen together at the hotel bar after the annual meeting broke up."

"You didn't make that up, did you, Doyle?" Tommy said. "Just because Meg's on your case for spending the organization's money like a drunk sailor."

"Not anymore," Ryan said. "I stopped submitting purchase requisitions. I'll be damned if she's going to make my life miserable."

"So Meg and Larry, huh?" Tommy said.

Ryan laughed and shook his head with a mixture of pleasure and disbelief.

Tommy laughed. "Maybe she likes tizzuns," he said.

I'd never heard the term tizzun until I met Tommy DiTullio. Though I was Sicilian by background and had heard Italian spoken during my childhood, usually at family gatherings at my grandparent's house, the only term for blacks that I could recall was mulignan. Blacks were eggplants, or rather the color of eggplants. Mulignan did not have the raw racism of the word nigger. It was, to me anyway, simply a descriptive term. It was like referring to a black person as being black or a white person as being white. Tommy also seems to have regarded mulignan as a racially neutral term. I heard him use it on more than one occasion with a black attorney who was one of his buddies from his old city hall days. But Tommy never used the term tizzun, which was obviously pejorative, obviously racially charged, in front of his old city hall buddy. He did use it liberally in front of me and Ryan and some of the other male staff, and he would often use it in public, glibly and mischievously certain that no one would know what it meant.

Once, when we were being seated at a crowded restaurant for lunch—Tommy, Ryan and I—Tommy blurted out in a tone loud enough for most of the diners in the room to hear: "Look at the size of the sandwich that tizzun has!" The man he was referring to, who was seated at the table next to us, never looked up, and never said a word. On another occasion—again it was Tommy and Ryan and I—we walked into an athletic complex, and halfway down the main hallway was a black maintenance man in workmen's clothes. Tommy, looking for directions, called out to the man, "Hey, tizzun!"

Tommy could be just as coarse and insensitive with whites. I remember taking him to one of my Rotary Club lunches, and after we went through the buffet line and sat at a table by ourselves, one of the Rotarians who had been behind us in line came up to us, plate in hand, and very amiably asked if he could join us, to which Tommy said, laughing mischievously, "Sure cornute. Have a seat cornute." Tommy could not say the word, which means cuckold in English, just once; he had to twice give this courtly gentleman what the Italians call "the horns."

I never heard Tommy use the word nigger. Then again he had a perfectly acceptable equivalent in tizzun. For Tommy's generation, born before and after WWI, the supposedly "greatest generation" for its patriotism and courage, the question of race did not trouble them as long as blacks were invisible. But racism was certainly part of their worldview. In my own growing up I did not hear much made of the issue of race, though I did hear and say the word nigger in a an old British counting rhyme that we used to recite: "eeny, meeny, miny, moe, catch a nigger by the toe, if he hollers, let him go, eeny, meeny, miny, moe." This counting rhyme is still recited today, but it is now "catch a tiger by the toe." My own experience with white people of my generation tells me that the term nigger has gone out of our lexicon, certainly out of the public lexicon. Black dignity and moral indignation have removed it from the vocabulary of the baby boomer generation and even more thoroughly from the generations that have followed the baby boomers. It is word that I never used publicly or privately, and one that Ryan Doyle never used publicly or (as far as I know) privately.

But why did Ryan and I tolerate Tommy's racial epithets? Was it because we knew he wasn't serious? Was it because we knew Tommy genuinely liked Larry Miller and other blacks with whom he was friends? Was it because we knew Tommy felt a sense of solidarity with the black community, a community like that of the Italians and of the Poles and of the Russians that had to ally itself with other groups to counter the power and money and influence of suburban WASPS like Peter Matthews? Probably. But that does not excuse my acquiescence. Fairness, one of the universal principles of ethics to which I am personally committed and to which my agency is committed, should have prompted me to say, "I don't think you should be using that term, Tommy." But I did not. Nor, to my knowledge, did Ryan Doyle. And our acquiescence on the issue of race would become a wound we could not heal.

Board Alignments

What I should have done was wage war on all factions, while aligning myself with the independents.

There were other reasons we were not critical of Tommy. He had a hold on us that was unbreakable, intractable, and a temperament attuned to the tiniest slight. If he could not effortlessly command a majority of the votes on the board of directors, he could effortlessly count on a substantial minority. But a majority was not out of the question either. Tommy had no peer when it came to organizational politics. He had no peer when it came to counting the votes. Tommy may not have been the titular president of the board, but he was, at least early in Larry Miller's tenure, the nominal president. And Tommy was a "president" whose touchiness meant that he was easily offended and, therefore, would not magnanimously accept any criticism or diminution of his power. I had made the mistake that many non-profit CEOs make: I had aligned myself with one faction of the board over another. What I should have done was wage war on all factions, while aligning myself with the independents.

Staff Alignments

When an institution is divided, no amount of competence can make it flourish.

I would take a different approach to factional infighting with the staff. By relying on the iron will of Evelyn Wagner, I had already rooted out one factional division among the staff. Another would emerge. This time along gender lines. The men lined up with Ryan Doyle, the women with Meg Michalsky. I could not tell at first from which camp the divide emanated.

Ryan Doyle was a single guy in his early thirties who did not have the most liberated view of women. In his view the feminist movement had soured relations between men and women, and he thought that our organization would be more effective if it had remained all boy as it had been since its founding in 1895, until the 1970s when girls were admitted into membership. The co-ed approach had, in Ryan's opinion, made our work with kids unnecessarily complicated, particularly with teenagers. He was right. It was more complicated. But it was fairer. We would eventually compromise on this issue and organize our program so that it was largely co-ed but also had single-gender activities. What I liked about Ryan was his work ethic. I would later learn that his other attribute was loyalty. But at this point in time I was not sure if Ryan's relationships with female staff were strained by an anti-feminist bias or if the female staff were being incited against him by Meg. What was clear is that Ryan was harried by his dealings with the detail-oriented Meg Michalsky.

At the time, our organization had a budget of less than a million dollars, and Meg Michalsky had the dual role of office secretary and finance director. With a work ethic to match Ryan's and an attention to detail that was exceptional, Meg made it clear she wanted more responsibility.

"I could do Ryan's job better than he does," she said to me one day as we sat across from each other at the conference table in my office. What she did not say that day and what I would soon discover was she was already confiding to others that she could also do my job better than I.

"But you never worked with kids," I said.

"Neither does he."

"He did, though. And in certain disciplinary cases, he still does."

"He's disorganized and you know it. He does everything by the seat of his pants."

"How do you know that?"

"Just talk to the staff," she said. "They'll tell you."

"They're telling you?"

"Not exactly."

"Then how do you know this? Who's saying it?"

"Well it isn't the bro's," she said, a term she had begun using to describe some of the male staff in the organization, especially the staff Tommy had nicknamed, the staff closest to Ryan Doyle.

"Then who is?"

"Forget it," she said, teary-eyed, a melancholy moment imminent.

"Okay. But I have to tell you, I don't see director of operations as a good fit for you, Meg. You don't have the background for it. You don't have the right education. You don't have the right experience. Fundraising is another matter. That might be something we could consider. Now, let's go over this financial statement."

My meetings with Meg about the monthly financial statements were always brief but pointed: I asked for additional information; Meg provided it. If our receivables were high, I would ask what they comprised of. Were the payables all current? Why was revenue for the month lower than projected? And if I found an error, I would offer the correction verbally; never in writing. On this particular statement, I noticed that membership revenue seemed particularly low year-to-date.

"It's accurate," Meg said.

"It suggests that our membership is down, which the board would not be very pleased with."

"That's what disorganization gets you."

"How about the revenue from the school district," I said. "Part of that revenue paid for memberships for all the kids in the basketball league. Did that revenue get posted to membership?"

"No, it didn't."

"Why not?"

"If that's what you want me to do, that's what I'll do."

"That's what I want you to do."

"Maybe the truth of the matter is," she said, "membership is down."

"The kids who participated in the league are all members. They were issued memberships. They participated in a sports program we developed and implemented. That **fact** ought to be reflected in our financial statement."

"That's misleading," Meg said.

Indignant, I said, "Misleading?!"

"Those kids don't come to the Agency. They play basketball in an elementary school gymnasium on Saturday afternoons."

"Even if they don't come to the Agency," I said, my hand chopping the air for emphasis, "they're still members. Not all of our programs are conducted in this building. Besides, how do you know they're not coming here?"

"Well, I wouldn't ask Ryan Doyle and his bro's. They're sure as hell not going to tell you the truth."

I stood up to signal that my meeting with Meg was concluded. She gathered up the financial statement in front of her, said, "I'll make the change in the membership revenue," and walked out of my office. Without knowing it then, I had just added another charge to be leveled against me: financial malfeasance.

Shortly after that, I added fundraising to Meg's portfolio of responsibilities, elevating her compensation and her stature in the organization. By promoting her, I made it appear that my loyalties lay with Meg's side of the staff divide. I made it appear that Meg, not Ryan, was now the number two staff person in the organization. But appearances can be misleading. What I had actually done was give an overly ambitious staff person an equally ambitious chart of work, much like I had done with the ambitious Matt Mihalak. If Meg succeeded, the organization would benefit; if she did not succeed, the organization would also benefit from her departure.

But I could not, for the moment at least, reveal to Ryan Doyle the full implications of my strategy with Meg Michalsky; the inclination to tell other staff would be irresistible to Ryan, and I could not afford to lose the leverage I had over Meg and over her future in the organization. I was not just testing Meg's vaulting and over-reaching ambition; I was also testing Ryan's loyalty. And however much Meg's promotion disappointed Ryan—and he did distance himself from me for a while—nothing he said or did in this period had a hint of disloyalty. What Meg Michalsky's promotion actually allowed me to do was choose a loyal diamond-in-the-rough over a highly competent intriguer. The lesson I would learn is that loyalty unites and intrigue divides; and when an institution is divided, no amount of competence can make it flourish.

Visionaries

All institutional visionaries must ultimately understand and defeat the Machiavellians in their midst.

After meeting with Meg Michalsky about the financial statements, I got up from the conference table, closed the door to my office and plopped down on the sofa where Tommy DiTullio customarily sat. I was too agitated to go on to the next task. In the sundry life of a non-profit CEO, there is always another task to do. If not evaluating existing staff, interviewing prospective staff. If not attending a community event, serving on a community committee. If not checking the background of a prospective board member, asking a member of the board to open the door to a donor. There is letter-writing, thank-you writing, grant writing, and report-writing. There are calls to make, calls to return; emails to write, emails to return. There are program issues, personnel issues, facility issues. Budgets to develop and budgets to manage. Money to raise and marketing to be done. Problems to solve. Decisions to be made. Financial statements to review. One could easily get lost in the multiplicity of tasks required of the CEO of a non-profit. But I remembered something Richard Roth, my old department director at the international office, told me shortly before I left the international organization to take a job in Syracuse, NY. It was something he should have told me my first day on the job rather than my last, because it was one of the best pieces professional advice anyone has ever given me. He warned me about the sundry nature of being the CEO of a local non-profit, and advised me that I should "always concentrate on one or two, maybe three, big ideas." Richard Roth was saying think big, not small; think strategically, not tactically; look forward, not backward. He was saying be a thinker, an innovator, a visionary. What Richard Roth did not tell me is that one cannot realistically forge a vision of the future without the political acumen to realize it. All institutional visionaries must ultimately understand and defeat the Machiavellians in their midst: those ruthless self-centered souls whose primary motivation is the acquisition of power.

And I did have a good command of the three big ideas Richard Roth thought one should have: lifting whole generations of kids to the level of civic engagement not seen since the founding of our nation; creating an exceptional staff based on liberally educated talent rather than on contemporary skill sets and middling credentials—a staff that fit Thomas Huxley's axiom that one ought to "know something about everything and everything about something;" and the idea that kids and staff and even the board ought to aspire to live what the ancient Greeks thought of as the good life, the admirable life, the ethical life. But there were two conjoined political dynamics diverting me from this tripartite vision: a staff divided along gender lines, and a board which was primed for political mischief. At the center of the staff divide stood Meg Michalsky.

An Age of Metrics

The nonprofit world, which has increasingly mimicked the for-profit world, is in the thrall of quasi-science, of metrics and skill sets.

My first misstep with Meg Michalsky had been to hire her when my intuition told me otherwise. But in an age of metrics, objective analysis has become the preeminent guide to executive decision-making. In the new age of reason—insight, intuition, and reflection—have all gone the way of the humanities in the modern university: to the lowest position of public acceptance. Social science, as Alan Bloom observed, has been elevated to the second position behind pure science, even though social science, if one can call it a science, can only produce quasi-scientific results. So the nonprofit world, which has increasingly mimicked the for-profit world, is in the thrall of metrics and skill sets. In the selection of employees like Meg Michalsky one is inclined, therefore, to concentrate on her skills, which are easier to analyze, and to ignore her personality, which even after two interviews might be better grasped by using one's intuition.

What I had intuited from my first interview with Meg was this: a personality as dour as hers could cast a pall over a small nonprofit organization, but an objective analysis of her skill sets indicated that she was someone who could do the work exceptionally well. However, as is often the case, her personality transcended her skills, and her technical competence was overwhelmed by her willfulness, her melancholic moods, her gossiping, and her active undermining of me and of Ryan Doyle. Her competence was further compromised by her overarching ambition, by her unbending belief that, in addition to running the office (her job), she could run the program (Ryan's job), run the organization (my job) better than we could. Meg Michalsky was the dark energy of the organization: paradoxically formidable yet weak, supremely competent yet unaccountably reckless. The women on staff admired her. The men feared her. And no one came to fear her more than I.

Executive Indecision

My indecision provided the perfect opportunity for my critics on the staff to align themselves with my critics on the board.

After hiring Meg, my next major misstep was to allow the division among the staff to go on as long as it did. Factional disputes among staff should not be thought of as congenial competitions that ultimately yield positive results, but rather as organizational divides that have debilitating results. Unlike a divided board, a nonprofit CEO cannot crush both sides of a staff divide without inciting the board to intervene. I had done that coming into the organization. I would not be able to do it again. And in the case of a small organization of thirty employees, there may not be much of a non-aligned staff group with whom to align. The obvious solution to this staff division would have been to eliminate its source: Meg Michalsky.

In time I realized that Meg was at the center of the staff divide, and I was sure that Ryan Doyle had made matters worse by his open disdain for Meg's coterie of discontented female staff. I tried to tell Ryan not to telegraph his contempt for Meg's female friends. I told him it was always better that your adversaries not know what you think of them. Then you have the tactical advantage of surprise if you have to make a move against them.

But rather than make a move against Meg directly, I made my move indirectly by creating a new position for her that included some of her former duties with added fundraising responsibilities. By playing to her pride and ambition—two qualities of character that superseded her abilities—I laid the foundation for her defeat. Still, I had not followed Machiavelli's advice, which was to kill one's enemies quickly, decisively, ruthlessly. I hesitated, and my indecision provided the perfect opportunity for my critics on the staff to align themselves with my critics on the board. I provided the perfect opportunity for Meg and her faction to join forces with Larry Miller and Tommy DiTullio.

Keeping Your Friends Close

I kept more rather than less distance between me and my enemies.

The fact that forces were gathering against me first came to my attention in a phone call from Chuck Lauer, a former vice president of the board. Chuck had been a board vice president brought on by Peter Matthews, but had stayed on after Peter and the other members of that leadership group left the board. Chuck even stayed on the board after Tommy asked him (at my instigation) to step down as vice president of the board, which he graciously agreed to do. But Chuck Lauer also was one of the board volunteers particularly captivated by Matt Mihalak's program abilities, and even more than his patron Peter Matthews, had a tendency to push his inquisitiveness about financial and budgetary matters too far. Because of Chuck's connection to Matthews and Mihalak and because I thought he was disproportionately inquisitive, I kept a cool distance from him. Tommy's advice regarding Chuck Lauer was that I ought to keep my friends close and my enemies closer, but I did not regard Chuck as an enemy, nor was I completely comfortable with him either. I preferred to rely on the example of Julius Caesar, the greatest leader from classical antiquity, who kept his enemy Brutus closer than he should have. As a result, I kept more rather than less distance between me and my critics. I did watch Chuck and others like him, but I watched them from a distance. If they were not on the board, I would veto any suggestion to put them on. And if they managed to make their way onto the board, I would make sure they did not become officers or committee chairs. They could be doers, donors or door-openers, but never decision-makers.

I hesitated a moment when I heard it was Chuck Lauer on the line. A call from him was unusual. But Chuck was a good door-opener. I thought maybe he was calling about some opportunity.

"Hi, Chuck. What can I do for you?"

Chuck always came quickly to the point. "Michael, I called to tell you about a situation I believe you should be aware of."

His tone told me that the situation was not an opportunity. "Okay," I said.

"Are you aware of a by-laws committee that was put together by Larry Miller?"

"This is the first I heard of it," I said.

"I thought that might be the case," he said. "I wondered why you weren't there."

"The committee has already met?"

"At my office," Chuck said. "Lenny asked me to host it."

"Who's on this by-laws committee?"

"Larry, Tommy, Maria DiSanto, Bobby Hathaway, Ed Bolden, and Connie Santone."

My baccala buddies from the Christmas luncheon. "This meeting was about by-laws?" I said.

"Maybe that was the original intention, but we never talked about by-laws. The meeting revolved around concerns that Larry has about you."

"What concerns?"

"I think you need to talk to Larry about that. I called you because I think you should be aware of what's going on. That's only fair."

"Can you tell me this? Were these concerns coming from everybody?"

"Larry for the most part. Maybe Tommy. Larry kept looking to Tommy to confirm what he was saying. Some questions were asked. I can't speak for anybody else, but I know I was hearing this stuff for the first time."

Restraining Presidential Power

I wanted to restrain the appointment power of the board president by requiring super majority approval of the full board.

I thanked Chuck, hung up the phone, and sat down on my sofa. I had to collect myself before I called Larry Miller. I had to reflect for a moment on what had happened. The first thing I noted was my circumstance was like that of my old friend Jimmy McNally: a committee meeting in secret to oust the agency CEO. By Chuck Lauer's account, Larry Miller's supposed by-laws committee meeting was attended only by board members. In one way this action was even more brazen than the secret personnel committee meeting designed to topple Jimmy McNally. Larry Miller had not just secretly convened a standing committee of the board; he had created an entirely new ad hoc committee without the CEO's knowledge and without the approval of the board. As board president Larry had the authority to create almost any committee he wanted, but he could not create it, according to our constitution, without board approval. That was the check, the balance of power built into our constitution and by-laws. Our constitution only required a president to seek a simple majority to approve his creation of a new committee or his appointment of board volunteers to specific committees. I made a mental note to change our constitution when the opportunity presented itself. I wanted to restrain the appointment power of a board president by requiring super-majority approval of the full board to create a committee or to appoint someone to a committee. I would later be convinced of the need for a super majority when I witnessed the mischief caused by Larry Miller's wholesale reorganization of all of the board committees late in his presidential term.

When and What for Committees Meet

Politically astute CEOs always decide when and what for committees meet.

Then I did what Tommy DiTullio taught me: I started counting the votes. I was fairly certain—one can never be entirely certain how a board member will vote—that Larry Miller did not have the votes to approve the creation of a by-laws committee, particularly if it was simply a ruse to topple me. He had also violated the principle in our constitution that called for the executive to be ex-officio on all committees and task groups. All non-profit CEOs should insist on being ex-officio members of all committees, standing and ad hoc, and all task groups, and they should further insist that this membership be written into the agency's constitution clearly and incontrovertibly. If CEOs cannot find the time to serve on all of their agency's board committees, then the agency has too many committees.

The rule for standing committees should be the fewer, the better; three at most; and for ad hoc committees and task groups: the fewer meetings, the better. A CEO can include other staff on board committees, but should never delegate serving on such committees to others. Volunteer chairs of board committees ought to have a role in shaping the agendas of their respective committees, but politically astute CEOs always decide when and what for board committees meet. These same CEOs know that all meeting notices must be sent out by the office of the agency, not the office of the volunteer. Once board volunteers start booking their own board committee meetings, CEOs become more vulnerable to being excluded from the kind of secretive meetings organized by the likes of Larry Miller and Tommy DiTullio.

The Job of President

Equally ominous was his view
that the presidency was a job
and that his job was not to lead but to manage.

In a crisis it was always my custom to call my mentor, Patrick McSweeney, who was not in. I called Jimmy McNally, but he was not in either. So I called Larry Miller, who was in, and he agreed to meet me at his office that afternoon. When I arrived at the offices of the public utility where Larry had worked since he got out of college, I gave my name to the receptionist and a few minutes later Larry came down to the lobby to meet me. We did not go up to Larry's office this time. It was not much of an office anyway, just one cubicle among many made up of portable partitions and office furniture that looked like it had come from a second-hand store. Instead we went into a cramped and unadorned conference room just off the lobby, and we sat across from each other in folding chairs at a small portable table. This was one public utility that was not wasting the public's money on extravagant office furnishings.

I thought about the last time I came here to meet with Larry. Usually we met at my office. On that occasion I told him about a major gift we just secured for our capital campaign from a retired CEO of a major company.

"You met with him?" Larry had asked. "Or did he respond to a letter?"

"No, we met with him."

"Who's we?"

"Brian Billingsley and I met with him."

Brian Billingsley was a partner in a major law firm, a labor lawyer who was the immediate past president of our board. Brian's presidency had been the most productive and least divisive of my tenure as CEO. His presidency had been marked by consensus and collegiality and by one striking accomplishment: the forging of a new strategic direction that led to our launching an ambitious capital campaign. As past president, Brian Billingsley was still playing a key role in securing major gifts for the campaign.

At the mention of Brian's name, Larry's

shoulders sagged and his face folded into a frown. "Why didn't you ask me to go on the call?" he said in an aggrieved rather than accusatory tone.

"He was on Brian's list," I said.

"I know Tom, too," Larry said, referring to the donor.

"Larry, we got the gift. That's all that counts."

"You always have to go to Brian Billingsley. Every time I turn around, you're going to Brian Billingsley. I'm the president of the board, not Brian. I'm smart. I can do these things just as well as Brian."

"I've gone to Brian on personnel matters," I said. "He's a labor attorney, Larry."

By personnel matters I meant policy matters, particularly revisions of our employee handbook. I had long ago stopped going to Brian Billingsley about employees with whom I was having difficulty. Labor lawyers are an invaluable asset on any board of directors, but it is wise to limit their agency involvement to policy making. Asking them to do more is an invitation for them to meddle in management. Instead I had begun using a partner of Brian's, who, when it came to employee problems like those presented by Meg

Michalsky, advised me not as to what I ought to do—as the board member in Brian tended to do—but rather presented the options open to me.

"I know what Brian is," Larry said, now more displeased than aggrieved. "But he's not the president anymore. I am."

"Yes, you're the president, but that doesn't mean I can or should run everything by you before I decide to do something. I have a job to do."

"So do I," Larry said firmly, as if issuing a warning.

I let Larry's admonishment that day be the last word. There seemed little likelihood that I would win the argument anyway. I could not convince a man so unsure of himself that the accomplishments of his predecessor were no threat to him. Larry Miller had the same curious combination that Tommy DiTullio had. He was an insecure man who longed for superior recognition. Equally ominous was his view that the presidency of the organization was a job, and that his job was not to lead but to manage. And he was by his own overly sensitive account smart enough to do just that.

The Coming Coup

If people come to me with concerns, I can't ignore them. I have an obligation to investigate them.

Seated across from him now, in a room so stark as to be grim, I asked Larry Miller what his so-called by-laws committee was all about.

In vintage community-speak, Larry said, "There are concerns that we need to address."

"By reviewing by-laws?" I said.

"If people come to me with concerns, I can't ignore them. I have an obligation to investigate them."

"So anyone can say anything they want to whoever they want, and you will investigate it?"

Larry looked down, stone-faced and silent.

"Wouldn't that responsibility fall to the personnel committee?" I said, knowing that the committee was chaired by Brian Billingsley, and had on it board volunteers who were either favorable to me or would at least be fair-minded and independent.

"We talked about that," Larry said. "about referring it to the personnel committee."

"Your by-laws committee decided this."

"Yeah," he said, grudgingly, uncomfortably.

"Larry, you can't just start creating committees on your own."

"I didn't create the personnel committee."

"But you did create a by-laws committee."

Larry nodded, but said nothing.

"To consider some concerns raised about me?" I said. "What concerns? And who's raising them?"

"A lot of people," he said, and although he did not tell me who, I could deduce many of the sources from the nature of the allegations. Later on I would get a detailed memorandum from Bobby Hathaway laying out all of the allegations. Bobby, who practiced corporate not labor law, nevertheless became Larry Miller's counselor and investigator in this matter.

It was alleged that I had deceived the board by inappropriately altering a financial statement. I knew that that allegation had come from Meg.

That I used an agency vehicle for personal use had also come from Meg.

I was accused of charging non-business food and beverage expenses to my organizational expense account. Meg again.

I supposedly had staff paint my house while on the agency clock. That had clearly come from Tommy.

The most troubling allegation—that racial epithets were routinely used by staff to describe Larry Miller—was leveled against me and Ryan Doyle. The specific allegation was that Ryan and I were going around town referring to Larry as a "stupid nigger." I thought at first that this was another made up allegation from the Machiavellian mind of Tommy DiTullio. It was actually the work of an ex-staff member named Heather Karnes. Heather, who clearly had been under the conspiratorial spell of Meg Michalsky, wrote a letter to Larry Miller that made its way to the full board and ultimately to me. What follows are excerpts from the letter. I have left out some of the references to Ryan Doyle.

"Dear Larry Miller,

I am writing about the information you requested about my experience with the Youth Association. When I was still working for the Association, my then supervisor, Bill Hager, and I had been discussing the problems at the Association. He encouraged me to call you and talk to you about the goings on there. He told me to tell you that Ryan Doyle and Michael Palermo used racial slurs against you and other non-white persons. Specifically, they called you a stupid nigger, and would make fun of you and imitate you. I told Bill I never heard this. Bill said he had. I personally never heard them talk like this about people or about you. Bill Hager would keep asking me if I were going to call you or someone on the board about my concerns, during the last two weeks of my employment. He kept encouraging me to do it. I feel Bill Hager was either setting me up to be a snitch or he was told to do this by someone else. He even said he was going to do it himself. He told me not to worry; he was going to take care of this himself. He was going to get his wife or a friend to call the board anonymously and tell the whole story. He also said if I told anyone he would deny it. I feel Bill was collecting information about my opinion and reporting back to Ryan and Michael. I also feel that Ryan and Michael feel that I am a stupid woman who knows nothing. Ryan Doyle does not have a very high opinion of women. He especially hates women in authority. One of the last things I said to Bill Hager was that I was not going to the board. I would talk if someone approached me. I said this in the (department) office. I said it loud and I also said this to (a) co-worker. I did this because I felt at the time that the office was bugged. I have no proof of this but it was a feeling I had. If the office was not bugged, then Bill Hager was their little reporter. Things got out that were only said in the office between my co-workers and myself."

I was astonished by the reckless manner in which Heather Karnes spread rumors about me and Ryan Doyle. Anyone who promulgated rumors this pernicious while professing to have no direct knowledge of them had no integrity at all. Then to pass the rumors on from someone whom you then discredit as an administration informant was astoundingly idiotic and unfair. Add to that the wildly conspiratorial notion of being bugged, and you have an accuser who has absolutely no credibility. But to Larry Miller, a man sensitive to the smallest slight—and this was clearly no small slight—Heather Karnes was credible.

I was stunned, angry, outraged. I wanted to sue everyone responsible for making these outrageous allegations, particularly Heather Karnes, who made the most egregious allegation of all. I was certain that my reputation was ruined. I was certain that, as with my friend jimmy McNally years before, these scandalous circumstances could only be accommodated by a dignified departure. It would take the good judgment of Patrick McSweney to persuade me otherwise. It would take the tenacity of my daughter Diane, the loyalty of Ryan Doyle, and the unfailing support of Brian Billingsley to prevail over a palace coup that reduced truth-telling to travesty and fairness to farce.

5

Coup

Honesty hath no fence against superior cunning.
~Jonathan Swift

Flee or Fight

My choices were to flee or fight.
There was no third way, no compromise,
no common ground.

Anger and indignation were my first reactions to the reckless allegations leveled against me. Then, diminished by rumor and political intrigue, I felt a deep sense of loss not unlike the grief one feels for the death of a loved one. I wanted to quit. I wanted to walk away. I wanted to start over. But Patrick McSweeney and Jimmy McNally reminded me that I could not go without setting straight that which DiTullio and Miller and Michalsky ruthlessly tried to re-write: the truth.

But why continue in this particular job in this particular organization in this particular town—especially with people I now neither trusted nor respected? Was it not ultimately about reputation rather than truth? And why attempt to regain—if indeed that were possible—something as ephemeral and insubstantial as one's reputation? As I considered this conundrum carefully, I was reminded of the advice the Roman philosopher and stoic Epictetus would have given: that a reputation, a job, a house, a neighborhood, a hometown—all of these things were ultimately out of one's control; the only thing one could truly control was one's mind, the thoughts occupied by one's mind, and the actions one took based upon those thoughts. But as much as I admired Epictetus, as much as I liked the life of the stoic and the life of the mind, I could not accept the fate that my critics had laid out for me.

So I gave more thought about why I wanted this particular CEO position. My first thought was that a nonprofit CEO position here was like any other CEO position somewhere else. The problem was that this particular "somewhere else" was where I really wanted to be. I was certain that leaving this position would require me to take whatever job I could quickly find—I had a mortgage to meet, tuition to pay, a line of credit to contend with—and I did not want to settle for a middle management job or even a senior management position in a larger organization.

I had started my career in this organization, left it for more than a decade, then came back as its CEO. I had been a member of this venerable organization as a child, just as my father and his brothers had been a generation before. I wanted to remain a CEO, and I wanted to remain the CEO of the local Youth Association.

This Pennsylvania city, known more for its pizza than pate, for its flats and frame homes on working class streets than its luxurious lake shore homes and stylish suburbs, for its child poverty than its natural beauty, for its family fare than its flourishing performing and fine arts, was so much in my marrow I could not conceive of leaving it.

I had made my daughter Diane leave this place when she was a child so I could pursue a professional ambition, taking her from the calm and quiet of an old Erie neighborhood to what we half-jokingly called the mean streets of Yonkers, New York. I did not want to do that again with my younger daughter Melissa, who seemed to be living the kind of idyllic childhood my wife and I remembered, a childhood characterized by a salutary school nearby, felicitous friends up and down the street, and a safe and tranquil neighborhood that was a special place of play.

If this had not been my hometown and if I had not had a long history with this particular nonprofit organization, I might have walked away. But as it was, my choices were to flee or fight. There was no third way, no compromise, no common ground. I had already seen friends and colleagues in less contentious circumstances decide to flee. I had seen them take severance packages that described their departures not as firings but as pursuits of opportunities. I could not accept such a disingenuous arrangement. Therefore, I could not and would not flee. I am if nothing else a contrarian willing to fight for principles, so walking away from a fight in which truth-telling and fair-dealing were about to be undone by political intrigue was not a course I could have taken. They wanted a fight. I would give them a fight. And the proper place to pick that fight, Patrick McSweeney advised me, would be before the full board.

"Most of the board knows nothing about this," Patrick said in one of our late night long-distance conversations, he with a glass of scotch and I with a glass of Tommy's homemade red.

"You've got to bring the rest of the board into this before they do. Put everything on the table, every single allegation, while you portray Tommy and his crowd as the reckless wing-nuts that they are. You do it to them before they do it to you. Then meet one-on-one with every single board member you think might be sympathetic, and every other one you think you can win over. Ultimately you want to expose this palace coup for what it is: a witch hunt designed to topple you and put Larry Miller in as the new CEO."

Patrick's plan was predicated on quick execution and sound strategy. The tactic to be executed was to counter the allegations quickly and decisively and, by doing so, win over the moderates and independents on the board before Larry and Tommy could compromise them. The long-term strategy was to portray my critics as reckless partisans engaged in a witch hunt. Although I trusted the political acumen of Patrick McSweeney, I was not particularly confident that I could accomplish either the objective or the strategy. With all the allegations already lodged against me, and more to be brought forward as the investigation widened, it would be a formidable task to persuade enough people on the board that virtually none of the allegations against me was true.

Even Brian Billingsley, a practicing labor attorney and past president of the board, quickly made clear to me that it was reasonable for the board to conduct an investigation into these allegations. So how would I characterize as a reckless witch hunt something that Brian Billingsley and (I assumed) others saw as a legitimate investigation? The Heather Karnes letter, which bordered on the bizarre, would help: Its twisted logic would provide a perfect foil, as would the over-reaching of Meg Michalsky, the complicity of Tommy DiTullio, and the lack of proportion to Larry Miller's leadership.

A Window into the Soul

Just as the ancient Greeks believed the eyes were a window into the soul, we moderns might consider writing a window into the human personality.

I made many mistakes in my handling of messers Miller and DiTullio—most notably my advocacy of the rise of Larry to the presidency of the organization and my complicity in making Tommy a nominating committee unto himself—but I did not recruit them to the board; I inherited them. In Meg Michalsky and Heather Karnes I had personally picked the two most troublesome employees I had ever encountered. I picked them based upon what I believed to be a thorough process with objective criteria. I picked them analytically rather than intuitively, while at the same time I was willing to stake the future of our organization on a strategic vision that was arrived at intuitively rather than analytically. Why wasn't I willing to use my intuition when I first encountered Meg Michalsky? I would not have hired her if I had followed my intuition. And what is the value of an analytical approach to the hiring process if someone capable of writing something as egregious as the Heather Karnes letter survives its scrutiny?

For most of my career I thought that business writing was a minor skill one could perform perfunctorily. I thought that writing passably well was sufficient for the kinds of correspondence a business career required. Even as someone whose background was in the liberal arts, I did not readily see the need for style or eloquence in the writing of letters or reports or grant proposals or remarks made to the local Lions Club. All one needed for this kind of writing was a modicum of clarity and simplicity. And in most circumstances, those two simple standards are sufficient. But there are two circumstances in which clarity and simplicity are not enough—in public speaking, and in reviewing the credentials of a prospective employee.

Any time CEOs stand in front of a group to speak, the community, or at least a segment of the community, will take the measure of the CEOs and the measure of the institutions which they represent. The audience will either be impressed or unimpressed or indifferent, and the only acceptable outcome for CEOs who want to be taken seriously as community leaders, who want to be thought of as having the kind of gravitas generally reserved for for-profit leaders, is for the audience to be favorably impressed. One eloquent and inspirational speech can transform an unknown nonprofit CEO into an admired and respected community leader, just as it had done on the national political stage for Ronald Reagan and Barack Obama. But simply writing well will not position one for that transformational moment. One must write eloquently and inspirationally, even if some ghost-writing is required to accomplish it. Nothing falls flatter than the reading of a well-written report. A stirring speech has an entirely different syntax than a report. It is written for the ear rather than the eye.

Just as the ancient Greeks believed the eyes were a window into the soul, we moderns might consider writing a window into the human personality. If I had had such a window to look through at Heather Karnes, I never would have hired her, which is why I would advise CEOs to ask for a writing sample from every prospective employee. To make sure that the writing sample is not ghost-written or edited by someone else, also require your applicants to write something extemporaneously as part of the interview process. Provide them with a set of facts, some related to each other, some not, and ask them to write a few paragraphs. This simple test will invariably reveal the clarity of their thinking and the nature of their personality. I would add to that an intelligence test and a personality profile. Hiring employees is the most important decision a CEO makes, and one should do it carefully and comprehensively. One should also do it intuitively as well as analytically. In hiring Heather

Karnes I was not comprehensive enough, not intuitive enough, not wise enough.

Loyalty Oaths

Loyalty of a cunning kind is stated strenuously, repeatedly, sycophantically.

Nor was I wise enough in hiring Bill Hager, who was now a source of one of the most serious allegations leveled against me. I do not think it was a coincidence that around this time Bill wrote a very revealing letter to the editor of the newspaper. My view about letters to the editor is that few of them are thoughtful enough to be taken seriously. Most of the letters published by in our local paper are the work of cranks and crackpots. Bill Hager's was in the crackpot category. In critiquing an article written by one of the editors of the paper (who happened to be Tommy DiTullio's nephew), Bill regaled the reader with some of the details of his supposedly illustrious career as a football player, prominently mentioning how he had come out of retirement to play the game he loved once again, only to reveal that that game he was referring to was not football, and certainly not professional football, but flag football. Had the letter been written with irony, it might have been comic and entertaining. Written straight-forwardly it came across as absurd. But Tommy did not take the criticism of his nephew lightly. He demanded that I fire Bill Hager. When I refused, Tommy insisted that I make Bill apologize to his nephew. I agreed to talk to Bill about it, but what I really wanted to talk to Bill Hager about was the Heather Karnes letter.

I made sure Ryan Doyle was with me when I met with Bill Hager. I wanted Ryan there to witness the encounter and give me his impressions. We met around the conference table in my office. I sat at the head of the table with Ryan on one side of me and Bill Hager on the other. I told Bill I had a letter I wanted him to read. I pushed Heather's letter across the table until it came to rest in front of him. Bill started to read it, but quickly became indignant. "Whoa, dude," he said, reverting to the street slang he often used. "I never said any such thing to Heather. No way I heard either of you guys ever say anything like that. No way. I heard Tommy DiTullio say stuff. I heard him refer to Larry as a tizzune. I heard him refer to Larry's privates as a roll of tarpaper.

But no way in hell you guys ever said anything like that about Larry Miller. And there's no way in hell I would ever say you did." Ryan and I had heard Tommy say the same things about Larry Miller.

"No?" I said.

"Absolutely not, dude. You guys know me. You know I'm loyal. Loyalty is always A number one with me, and you know that. I've always been loyal to you guys, and always will be."

"Why did she single you out?" I said.

"Beats me. Maybe it's because I'm her boss. Maybe it's because she spends too much time in Michalsky's office."

There was a pause in the conversation as Bill Hager read the rest of the letter.

"This is pretty far out stuff," he said, finally. "She thinks the office is bugged? And I'm setting her up? Man, that's out there." Then Bill turned to look directly at me and said, "Dude, just get me in front of Larry Miller and I'll tell him that this is all bullshit."

"You're willing to tell Larry that," Ryan said, glowering at Bill.

"Get him on the horn. I'll tell him right now."

"We'll do it face-to-face," I said. "I'll set it up."

Before leaving my office that day, Bill Hager again made mention of his unconditional loyalty to me and to Ryan.

"How many times did he say how loyal he was?" I said to Ryan after Bill walked out of my office.

"Seemed like every other word," Ryan said.

"Do you believe him?" I said.

"He said it so much it sounded like he was trying to make himself believe that he was loyal."

"So do you believe Heather was telling the truth when she said Bill told her that we were going around calling Larry a dumb you-know-what?"

"I don't believe either one of them," Ryan said.

"How about the reference to Heather spending all that time in Michalsky's office?"

"Couple that with the fact that every new female staff member eventually goes south on us? Why is that?" Ryan was being rhetorical. He already knew the answer.

But I said it for him anyway. "Meg is the fulcrum for all of this stuff. She's the one who branded us the bro's."

"And I think Bill is in deeper than we think," Ryan said. "If nothing else, he's waiting to see which way the wind is going to blow."

Bill Hager's loyalty oath was further proof to me that he was, as Ryan suspected, watching which way the wind was blowing; for real loyalty is quiet, active, exemplary; loyalty of a cunning kind is stated strenuously, repeatedly, sycophantically.

The next day we met with Larry Miller—Bill Hager and Ryan and I—in the small, stark meeting room off the main lobby of Larry's office building. The three of us sat on one side of the table and Larry on the other. We were three white men trying to persuade a black man that we had not referred to him in racist terms. It came down to Bill Hager to repair the rift. Bill was passionate and persuasive, and Larry said he accepted Bill's explanation. But the pained, puzzled look on Larry's face revealed a deep wound that would take more time to heal if it would ever heal at all.

Swift's Warning

I wondered whether truth could triumph over rumor.

I went on the attack a few days later when the full board met for its monthly meeting in the large conference room off the main lobby of our building. The board room was long and narrow, in the center of which was a conference table that could accommodate as many as thirty people. Twenty-two of the 35 members of the board attended the meeting that day—a typical turnout. I had always made it a habit to sit at the head of the table next to the board president—believing that it conferred on me a certain status as a leader equivalent to if not greater than the board president—but on that day, and every day after that, I sat at the head of the table opposite Larry Miller. After the preliminaries were performed—the call to order and the approval of the minutes of the last meeting—I asked for the floor, which Larry grudgingly granted.

"I wanted to take this opportunity to bring the full board up to date on some allegations that were made principally against me, but also against Ryan Doyle. Most of you have almost no knowledge of these allegations—except what you may have read in a letter by Heather Karnes—because you were not invited to the meeting at which they were apparently aired. Neither was I.

"It was a meeting convened at Larry Miller's request, a meeting of the by-laws committee. If you have not heard of the by-laws committee, that is understandable, since for all practical purposes there is no by-laws committee. At least no by-laws committee was properly proposed to and voted upon by the full board. And this so-called by-laws committee met not to discuss by-laws, which one might expect a by-laws committee to talk about, but rather to discuss concerns that have been raised about me and Ryan Doyle. Mostly, as I said, concerns about me.

"Let me first say that no one so far has told me specifically who made these allegations against me and Ryan, though the specific nature of the allegations are more than suggestive about who might be the actual sources. Not one of these allegations, which I would like to lay out for you now, not one, is true. Some of them lack even the scantest appearance of being true, and have clearly been made up whole-cloth, or fall into the category, as Heather Karnes' does, of spreading a rumor based upon a source even the accuser does not believe.

"Let me first address the financial allegation. I have never in all my years here prepared a financial statement, nor have I directed anyone, verbally or in writing, to change a financial statement so as to mislead the board about an aspect of our finances. If I directed our finance director to make a revision of our statement, it is because, after reviewing it, I found an error. I never directed Meg Michalsky, as is being alleged, to make a change that was knowingly inaccurate and knowingly intended to deceive.

"I did direct Meg Michalsky to take some school district revenue and re-post it to membership fees because part of that revenue was meant for that very purpose: buying memberships for kids in the basketball program that we run on the district's behalf. That is eight hundred kids at three dollars per kid (the cost of a membership) that I told her to move from school district revenue to membership revenue. There is absolutely no deception in that, no financial malfeasance.

"It has also been alleged that, while I have received a monthly car allowance as a part of my compensation, I have also been using one of the organization's vehicles for my personal use, in effect, double dipping. Even though Meg has encouraged me on a number of occasions to take one of our mini-vans home—purportedly because we would not have to pay a monthly parking fee for it—I only used a van to attend community events on behalf of the organization, and in some cases actually used it to transport people seated at this table."

I paused and took a long look at Larry. I wanted to name names. It would have made for an amusing of irony to say that my accusers were guilty of the same offense of which they were accusing me. But for the moment I preferred to pique the curiosity of the others in the room, a curiosity that I could later use to my advantage. Instead I went on to the next charge, one even more hypocritical.

"It has also been alleged that I used my expense account, which is budgeted at eight hundred dollars for the year, for personal rather than professional expenses. I do not recall ever using my expense account for personal expenses. I use it for an occasional business lunch or community dinner. If there are specific expenses that are being questioned, I have not received any notification concerning them. And some of the community events I attended were attended with people in this room."

Again, I refrained from naming names and from clarifying whether anyone in the room—the baccala boys (and girls) came to mind—had had their expenses paid for by the organization.

"Another allegation is that I had staff from the Agency paint my house. That is a total fabrication. No staff member has ever done any work for me at my house, painting or otherwise.

"And finally, it has been alleged that Ryan Doyle and I have been using racial epithets to describe Larry Miller. Some or all of you have already received a letter from a disgruntled former staff member, Heather Karnes, in which she makes this allegation. In the letter Heather admits that she never saw or heard either me or Ryan make any racial comments whatsoever, but that another staff member, Bill Hager, told her that we had made these comments. She goes on in the letter to discredit Bill Hager, whom she used as the source of the rumor she promulgated. She used as her source someone she did not trust, someone who has since told Larry Miller face-to-face that neither Ryan nor I ever made any racial comments in his presence. It is disconcerting to say the least that someone of Ryan's integrity should have his reputation besmirched by such a reckless allegation."

In the silence that ensued I wondered whether I had persuaded any of the moderates and independents on the board, and I wondered whether truth could triumph over rumor, whether it could survive the assault Jonathan Swift had warned about, of the superior cunning of human nature.

The Power to Prevail

I now knew that the power to prevail politically
lay not in persuading the crowd,
but in cultivating the individual face-to-face.

Larry Miller finally broke the silence by announcing that the personnel committee would continue its investigation into the allegations, and without further comment moved on to the next item on the agenda, which was whether we ought to join a state alliance of Youth Association organizations.

"I'm just not convinced that we should join this state alliance," Larry said as he opened the floor for discussion.

I had already made the case at two previous board meetings—convincingly, I thought—that we had no reason not to join the association, so I sat silently and waited to see if someone would challenge Larry's opinion. When no one spoke up in favor of the proposition, Debbie Watkins, who for the first time I could recall had seated herself next to Larry Miller and who had in fact moved her chair so that she was actually seated at the head of the table alongside Larry, did ask for the floor, but not to challenge Larry, to challenge me. In a tone that was strident if not indignant, Debbie asked me the same questions that had been asked and answered at the two previous board meetings—questions about incorporation and by-laws, about legal liability and local autonomy, and about cost.

While I was re-answering these questions, I could hear audible grumbling and sighs of frustration from board volunteers seated near me. I even heard one of them beleagueredly say, "Nothing comes easy in this organization." The support of these volunteers was heartening, but in view of their frustration I worried that they might not be able to sustain their support. I worried that some of them would resign and some would simply stop coming around. Debbie's last line of questioning concentrated on the cost of our participation in the state alliance. "Three thousand dollars is a lot of money to lay out in dues, without any assurance of getting anything in return," she said.

By this time I was agitated, or riled, as Brian Billingsley described my demeanor that day, and I said, "I could not disagree with you more. Three thousand dollars is a very small sum to invest when we can get tens of thousands of dollars in return."

"**Can** get," Debbie said. "That is vastly different than **will** get."

"Every other state association that has formed so far has ended up in the **will get** category, to the tune of a half a million to two to three million. Even if we were only able to secure half of the lowest amount so far raised from state governments, or two hundred and fifty thousand, that would be about a seventeen thousand dollar return on a three thousand dollar investment."

Just then I heard someone near me mumble that this was a "no-brainer."

"There are fifteen Youth Association organizations in the state," I said as I looked not at Debbie Watkins and Larry Miller but at everybody else in the room, "and the boards of fourteen of them—that is everybody but us—have already voted to be a part of this opportunity." Then I took a long hard look at Larry and Debbie and said: "If there was ever such a thing as a no-brainer, this is it."

In two weeks time I met with every member of the board I could meet with—not of course with Larry's and Tommy's loyalists—but with everyone I considered to be moderate and independent. A few of the moderates were openly sympathetic to my version of the events. Many more were at least skeptical of Larry Miller's motivations. And none of them was antagonistic to my protestations of innocence. A couple of the moderates did drift away and ultimately resign from the board. Maybe they were reluctant to be embroiled in something so politically unpleasant, or maybe they thought the situation might lead to litigation, but these individual meetings were productive and enlightening nevertheless.

I learned that I had enough support on the board to continue to challenge the allegations lodged against me. I found that face-to-face meetings with individual board members is something a non-profit CEO ought to do periodically as a matter of routine, rather than wait for a crisis to occur. I learned that judging board members on the basis of their behavior in meetings was a bad benchmark. Face-to-face I was able to find out positions on policy and on people that never got expressed in board meetings. I was able to forge if not friendships at least acquaintanceships that brought with them a richer mutual respect and understanding. And my meetings with the moderates gave me an insight into the political dynamics of the organization which I never before had and which I would need to prevail politically: I now knew where I stood in relation to each one of them, and where they stood in relation to each other. I now knew that the power to prevail politically lay not in persuading the crowd, but in cultivating the individual face-to-face. I was now ready to do what that old politico Tommy DiTullio had taught me to do: count the votes. But the counting would come later. I first had a date with another kind of destiny: my own mortality.

Leadership: The Universal Condiment

Leaders are fundamentally people with ideas who also have an intuitive touch for the big idea.

The day I stood unsteadily on the dividing line between life and death began without a hint of anything uncommon to come. I got up early to read and write, then showered, shaved and dressed. Rather than read the paper while I ate my breakfast, I left the house early because I was speaking at a breakfast meeting of a local civic group. When I spoke before one of these groups, whether it was the Rotary or the Kiwanis or the Lions or one of the many other civic groups in town, the usual expectation was that I would talk about the my organization for twenty minutes or so and then answer questions. But this group had asked for a bio in advance and, noticing that I had a background in leadership development, asked me to talk about young people learning to be leaders.

Actually it had been many years since I had worked with young people in programs that were designed to develop leadership, and over time I had come to reject those programmatic approaches—approaches, for example, in which

I had grafted group dynamic theory onto modern models like situational leadership—as not having any fundamental relation to leadership. The whole idea of leadership had become fertile ground for theorists of all kinds. Seemingly everybody on the planet believed that everything everybody did had its origin in an act of leadership. Leadership had become the universal condiment of our culture, so it was not coincidental that the only thing more ubiquitous than books about leadership were books about diets. Even my own national organization's fascination with executive development, after a brief flirtation with the idea that good executives were little more than an amalgam of requisite skill sets, would eventually grasp onto the executive leadership theory of University of Michigan professor Noel Tichy, a theory more pedagogic than gastronomic, in which the leader is not really a leader but rather a teacher. In fact, in Tichy's university (and universe) everyone, followers and leaders alike, are teachers and, therefore, leaders. And since I was a leader, by training and experience, but mostly, I think, by education, why not advance my own theory of leadership to these affable but bleary-eyed Rotarians: the leader as thinker.

I would borrow liberally to support my theory—from Archilochus, Isaiah Berlin and Jim Collins, from Thomas Huxley and Allan Bloom and from Noel Tichy himself. I told the Rotarians that what had been written about leadership was so abundant that it was difficult to define. One school defined leadership as a skill or set of skills, and the skill most often invoked was communication. A figure like Ronald Reagan could lead by his ability to communicate and thus was known as The Great Communicator. Another school defined leadership as a matter of having the right personal attributes. Washington was courageous in war, Lincoln steadfast about nationhood, Reagan fearless in defense of freedom. Like Berlin divided literature, I divided politics, categorizing Reagan a hedgehog, Clinton a fox, Lincoln a hedgehog, and FDR a fox.

But ultimately, I said, leaders must influence: they must touch people's hearts and change people's minds, and to persuade, especially to inspire, a leader, to borrow Thomas Huxley's definition of an educated person, "needs to know something about everything and everything about something." Bloom would have leaders delve even deeper than Huxley's breadth and depth of knowledge. He would have them reflect on what the greatest minds had written about the greatest ideas that were recurrent in every era of history. With credit to Collins and Tichy, I concluded my Rotarian remarks by arguing that leaders were fundamentally people with ideas who also had an intuitive touch for the big idea. But just as information does not readily conduce to ideas, ideas not reflected upon rarely conduce to wisdom. So in the non-profit world, where consensus requires a deliberation not always necessary in the corporate world, a CEO must above all be wise.

The thought of taking the essence of leadership beyond the realm of idea-maker into the broader realm of wisdom had not even occurred to me as I started to speak to the Rotarians that day. From where did this idea of leader as sage originate? From Alan Bloom? From Thomas Huxley? Or did it really go back much farther than that, to antiquity perhaps? These questions would continue to command my attention. I would continue to ponder them as one would expect an aspiring sage CEO to do, but another question was about to consume me, the question of my own mortality.

Life and Death

The contemplation of death's finality brought me back to death's corresponding pre-occupation: life, and how to live it.

My father had a heart attack and open heart surgery at forty-six, and he was gone at fifty-eight. From someone who once started a speech with the phrase "demographics are destiny" and whose curiosity led him to explore the genetic determinism of scientists like H.O. Wilson, I knew that genes could be destiny too. They could be, and were, my destiny. Of my three younger brothers, two made it out of their forties without having a heart attack, while one currently is perched precariously in his middle forties. I had a different destiny than my brothers. I had not lived as hard as my father had—he was born in December of 1929, just weeks after the Great Crash, and by age fourteen was working full-time for my grandfather's crew of plasterers. My father worked hard by day and sometimes played even harder at night.

Although I had done none of the things my father had done—my life had been safe and soft and privileged compared to his—I suffered the same fate: awaking at midnight of the day I had delivered the leader as sage speech with a pain in my chest that I had never before experienced. It was as if someone were sitting on my chest while driving the point of a pick into my sternum: it was a powerful pain, a pain paradoxically heavy and sharp. I woke my wife, who woke our eleven-year-old daughter, and after taking two aspirins and hurriedly dressing while hunched over in pain, I got into our car with my wife and daughter and we headed for the hospital. On the way to the hospital, my daughter Melissa dialed 911 and my wife Janice explained to the dispatcher that I was having a heart attack. An ambulance intercepted us about halfway to the hospital and transported me the rest of the way.

I remembered taking a ride like this with my father more than twenty years before. He was to meet us for a family picnic at the beach: a hook-shaped peninsula that juts out from the shore of the lake and forms on its north side a beautiful line of beaches stretching for several miles. I was standing on the crest of one of those beaches when I saw my father pull up and park on the side of the road below. As he started up the sandy rise to where I stood, I noticed two things that alarmed me: he was swaying slightly as he walked; and his olive skin had gone ashen. I knew then, as I ran down the beach to meet him, that my father was having a heart attack.

I was the one who drove him to the beach's first aid station a few miles down the peninsula road where an ambulance then took him to the hospital. He sat slumped in the seat beside me, his head resting on the top contour of the seat and angling to the side so that he was facing me. I alternately gazed at him and glanced at the road in the few minutes it took us to get to the first aid station. Lacking my mother's Nordic calm, I was, like my father, inclined to passion if not panic in a crisis. But there was none of that on that serene summer day. We were both strangely tranquil and uncommonly philosophical. Perhaps it was, as Samuel Johnson had observed, that the certainty of death concentrated the mind. It concentrated my father's mind on a topic he had never before brought up.

"What kind of father do you think I've been?" he said, his ashen face beaded with perspiration.

"You've been a good father," I said without hesitation.

"Is that what you really think of me?"

"Of course it is."

"I made my mistakes, but I always tried to do my best by you and your brothers and your mother."

"And you did your best."

"You think so?" he said, inviting me to elaborate.

The boy in me remembered a father colossal in scale, heroic—he was handsome, witty and energetic. He was loving and light-hearted. He was young—only eighteen when I was born—and full of optimism and a love of life. But more than life, he loved his children. He loved us unconditionally. But later, from a man's perspective, I saw him in a harsher light. I saw the colossal in him cut down to human scale. I saw his health fail and his optimism wane. I saw his humor and wit degenerate into sarcasm and discouragement. I saw a good father and fine family man fall into occasional bouts of drinking and infidelity. But in his loyalty to and his love of his children, he never wavered. And loyalty and love were, for me, what ultimately defined him.

"Dad, who knows whether we do our best or not," I said. "I only know that, no matter what we did, and we did some monumentally stupid things, you were always there when we needed you. That makes you the best of fathers. That makes you the kind of father whose love and support can always be counted upon. So if that's what doing your best is, then you did your best, and we love you for it."

An ambulance was waiting at the first aid station to take my father to the hospital. I followed him there as my wife and daughter would follow me more than twenty years later. He would have triple bypass surgery a few weeks later, and would live almost twelve years after the surgery, but we never again talked about our relationship in the way we did on that drive along the peninsula road. Even as his health declined and the end of his life was imminent, he never talked to me about his mortality, never hinted that he had had any reflections about his impending death. My guess is that he viewed death with a sense of dread. Or he viewed it not at all, but simply ignored it. Life was what really mattered to him, life that was lived in the moment, life that was lived with good food and drink, lived with laughter and tears, with song and dance, love and sex. But however much my father loved life—and he did love life, not only its physical pleasures of food and drink and sex, but its higher manifestations when he elevated his singing and dancing to forms of art—it never would have occurred to him to be philosophical about death. In that sense I was not my father's son. I was my own man. How much so would be revealed to me in my own encounter with death.

It occurred to me as I was transported to the hospital and as I lay on the examining table in the emergency room that the thought of dying just then was not at all troubling to me. I wondered why this was so. It certainly was not because my Catholic upbringing reassured me of a life after death. I viewed death as a definitive end. And I certainly did not entertain the notion, as many people stubbornly do, the well educated and uneducated alike, even those skeptically predisposed, that in death we will be reunited with loved ones who have gone on to immortality before us. I thought that perhaps the morphine they were giving me for pain had allayed any trepidation I might have had about dying. I also considered what Sherwin Nuland had written about endorphins in his blunt but brilliant book **How We Die**. Nuland's book made me think it was possible that my own brain was releasing these morphine-like substances called endorphins, which were then giving me a sense of tranquility to counterbalance the trauma of the heart attack.

At first the doctors and nurses in the emergency room were able to stabilize me, and the pain subsided a little. It was during this time that my oldest daughter, Diane, arrived at the hospital and spent a few tearful moments with me. In contrast to the doleful look on her face was an indignant tone of voice, a voice implacable in its belief that my heart attack had been caused by the machinations of DiTullio and Miller and Michalsky. The encounter with my daughter, like the fateful drive I took with my father many years before, made me realize that in a crisis people will reveal things about themselves that they would not otherwise disclose. It also made me realize that there was not, nor would there ever be, anyone as fiercely loyal to me as my daughter Diane.

When my condition worsened, they rolled me into the catheterization lab for an emergency angioplasty. The cardiologist who performed the catheterization had been called to the hospital for another patient whose symptoms subsided. But rather than go home, he went to a lounge, where, coincidentally, he just happened to be available a little while later to open an artery in my heart that had completely closed. Was this simply serendipity? Or was it something the fates, or should I say God, allowed? As someone who tended to stoicism, I could accommodate a concept of God as long as it did not require me to believe in the universally naïve notion that consciousness was eternal. So just as it had been my fate to have a heart attack, it was my duty to deal with it calmly and reasonably, even if it meant, as my cardiologist explained to me after the pain and pressure in my chest instantaneously stopped, that I needed open-heart surgery.

I was, as they say, harvested; meaning that the date of my surgery was set for three days hence. I remained in the hospital for recuperation purposes and for pre-operative testing. But early on the morning of the operation, my surgeon, a small, soft-spoken Filipino doctor with a reputation for prudence and perfection woke me to tell me that he wanted one more test performed: an echo cardiogram. As the doctor explained the need for still another test, my mind was occupied by something that seemed more remarkable: I had, on the eve of one of surgery's most invasive and painful procedures, slept soundly and serenely. Why was this so? I would, as it turned out, have plenty of time, weeks in fact, to ponder this question. The echo revealed that I had a blood clot in my heart, and it would take several weeks to dissipate it. So I went home, pondered my plight, and marked time.

What was time anyway? For physicists like Einstein, time as we know it is just an illusion. In a letter about the death of a fellow physicist, Einstein wrote that in "quitting this strange world, he now has gone a little ahead of me. This is of little significance. For us believing physicists, the separation of past, present, and future has only the character of an illusion." Near the end of his **Meditations**, Marcus Aurelius expressed a sentiment similar to Einstein's. He wrote "that everything which happens, always happened so and will happen so, and now happens so everywhere." Here we have a philosopher and emperor from classical antiquity arguing what modern physicists like Brian Greene have popularized: that relativity theory has demonstrated time is not linear, but rather that all of time, or what the great philosopher described as having happened and will happen and is happening now, exists. What was and what is and what will be, despite one's limited individual perspective, is (to use Greene's metaphor) a huge loaf of bread. And that loaf of bread not only was and will be, but is. So maybe our beloved Bill Clinton was right. It all comes down to what the meaning of **is** is.

Perhaps it was not so strange then that I found these scientific ideas about time and eternity, which I, of course, could only grasp in the most rudimentary conceptual way, comforting and reassuring as I contemplated my illness and impending operation. If I could not project my own consciousness, my own being, onto eternity and, therefore, anticipate a celestial reunion with family and friends, then at least could comfort myself with the fact that my family and friends and I would forever occupy slices of life in the great loaf of spacetime. And though as Marcus Aurelius once observed, "all things soon pass away and become a mere tale, and complete oblivion soon buries them," I was still reassured in the belief that since we once were, we would always be, however soon oblivion buried us.

In the weeks of waiting for my operation,

I read and re-read the **Meditations**. In reading this ancient text, which was originally written in Greek, I realized how unreservedly relevant and strangely modern was the wisdom of antiquity. I even told my wife that I thought every school-age child starting at the age of twelve ought to read the **Meditations** that year and every year thereafter. I told her this not because Marcus Aurelius more closely approximated Plato's idea of the Philosopher King than any leader in the history of the West. In fact, the great man's stoicism and its exhortation that one ought to "be mild and benevolent towards every man" may have prevented him from rising to the stature of the greatest of the Caesar's, Augustus and Julius. Perhaps he was not, in Machiavellian terms, ruthless enough; had he been so, his son Commodus never would have become emperor. But I found in his thought great wisdom and even greater comfort.

For the Stoics in general, death was something one constantly kept in the foreground, not out of some morbid curiosity, but because doing so sharpened one's appreciation of life. How long one lived was irrelevant to Stoics like Seneca and Marcus Aurelius. The only thing that mattered was how well one lived, and living well meant living rationally, dutifully, virtuously. Marcus Aurelius put it this way: "What is thy art? To be good." But to live the good life, the admirable life, also meant for Aurelius "waiting for death with a cheerful mind." Why? Because death was "nothing else than a dissolution of the elements of which every living being is compounded." Death, for the great man, was natural, as natural as the air we breathe. It was "according to nature." It was a dissolution, a scattering of atoms, of dust to dust. It was final. The contemplation of death's finality brought me back to death's corresponding preoccupation: life and how to live it and later, life as a nonprofit CEO and how to live that part of a higher life lived rationally, dutifully and virtuously. Or, in a word, how to live and work wisely.

Unlike most of my contemporaries, especially those whom I had encountered in my career as a nonprofit CEO, I had begun to notice late in my forties that my liberal arts background and my lifelong habit of reading classics more often than contemporary works had instilled in me a distinct pleasure in living what the ancient Greeks thought of as the life of the mind. Though the life of the mind that I was living was considerably less learned than the best minds of my generation and not even in the same solar system as the ancients and probably not on the same planet as the average college professor, I found in it and continue to find in it great joy. It is for me a form of the higher life for which I feel a deep and durable connection. And though there was nothing great in the way I was living the life of the mind, I shared in common with the great man himself, with the Roman world's Philosopher King, a reverence for rationality.

For Marcus Aurelius, "…the mind maintains its own tranquility by retiring into itself." Later in the **Meditations** he writes that "…the mind which is free from passions is a citadel, for man has nothing more secure to which he can fly for refuge…" One can see Plato here in the idea of the rational part of the soul reigning in the passionate. But Aurelius is saying something more about the reality around us: namely, that nothing in the outer world, nothing in the reality outside the mind, can harm us. Only our minds can cause us harm and only when we allow the passions to prevail. This is a wonderfully liberating thought. Aurelius himself wrote that we should begin each day with the understanding that we will "meet with the busybody, the ungrateful, arrogant, deceitful, envious, unsocial," but that none of them, not the envious Meg Michalsky, not the cunning Tommy DiTullio, not the aggrieved Larry Miller, can injure us, "…for no one can fix on us what is ugly…" Retreating to the citadel of one's mind seems eminently wise when dealing with life's busybodies and other minor irritants, but the great man may have gone too far when he advised living one's "life in truth and justice, with a benevolent disposition even to liars and unjust men." The misguided and the well-intentioned may be moved by benevolence, but the calculating and cunning are not so easily persuaded. It is doubtful that a benevolent disposition would have moved Larry Miller, for as soon as word got out that I had had a heart attack, he called an emergency meeting of the officers of the board to announce that in my absence he would be stepping in to manage the organization.

Private Support and Public Passion

CEOs must be content to seek support in private, while not expecting supporters to reveal their support in public.

Two days after my heart attack Ryan Doyle visited me at the hospital and told me everything he could recall of Larry Miller's emergency meeting—a meeting called so quickly (the day after my heart attack) that Ryan wondered if it had been pre-arranged.

"That had to be the fastest Larry ever moved in his life," Ryan said.

I had adjusted my bed, and was now sitting up. I laughed. "Yeah, the big guy has never been known for his swiftness."

Ryan relaxed a little. The anxious look on his face faded. He smiled. "What was that quote you used to describe Larry and Tommy? From Boss what's his name?"

"Boss Tweed. 'I saw my opportunities and I took 'em.'"

"That's what went down here," Ryan said. "Larry saw his opportunity with you out of the way, and he took it. Except you're **not** out of the way. But we can talk about that later, when you're feeling a little better."

"Ryan, I'm feeling fine; you can tell me what happened."

"Okay," he said, his uncertain look suddenly serious. "I had no idea this meeting was going down, but I knew something was up when I saw Michalsky hurry out the front door just minutes before board members, all the officers, start showing up. I don't think there's any doubt that Michalsky knew about the meeting and was supposed to be **in** the meeting."

"You have to wonder why he called the officers together," I said, "instead of his by-laws committee."

"Probably because you completely discredited that group at the last board meeting."

"So what happened then?"

"So everybody's there. They're in the conference room. I'm standing in the lobby at this point, and Miller's standing in the doorway of the conference room. About to close the door. So I walk up to the door like I'm going into the meeting and Miller stops me and says, 'You don't need to be in here,' and I just say, 'oh no' and push past him and go in and sit down."

"You literally pushed him out of the way?" I said, trying to picture Ryan, at 6'1" and 225 pounds, pushing past the much bigger Larry Miller, who is 6'9" and maybe 265 pounds.

"Yeah, I bumped him a little. But wait, there's more. We have another confrontation at the end of the meeting. Anyway, I go in and sit down like I belong in the meeting. Miller takes one last look into the lobby—probably wondering where Michalsky is—closes the door, sits down at the head of the table and starts the meeting. He starts out talking about the fact that you had a heart attack and can't perform your duties, and right away I jump in and say, 'No, Michael's fine. I talked to him this morning. He's perfectly capable of making any decision that needs to be made.'"

"What's everybody else doing at this point?" I ask.

"Nothing. They're not saying a thing. In fact, they're not even looking at Miller. They're looking down at the table. You can tell they're really uncomfortable."

"They eventually speak up, though, right?"

"No. Miller and I do all the talking. Miller goes on about how he needs to step in and run things in your absence, and I simply say, That's not necessary. I've got everything under control,' and it goes back and forth like that for a few more minutes, and the meeting ends on a sort of inconclusive note."

"So what happened then?"

"Everybody leaves except Miller—the rest of them can't get out of there fast enough—and

Miller's hanging in the lobby maybe thinking he's going to occupy your office. Maybe he's waiting for Michalsky, but she's nowhere in sight. And I'm not going anywhere. I'm determined to stay in that lobby until I get his ass out the door. Finally I kind of maneuver him into standing near the front doors and I just close in on him and push him out."

"You literally pushed him out the door."

"Yeah. I don't think he wants any part of me."

I laughed at this slapstick scene. I could not help but see something comic in Ryan nudging the man mountain out of the double doors and down the front steps of our building. But upon reflection the whole scene caused me more consternation than comic relief. The officers of the board, though they still privately supported me, were clearly disinclined to make their support public. Had they and others on the board been publicly passionate in their opposition to Miller's mischief—his reckless and unrelenting investigating and his transparent attempt to position himself as my replacement—a year of institutional paralysis could have been avoided. This was a difficult lesson to learn. Public passion is the last thing board volunteers will bring to an institutional crisis. CEOs must be content to seek support in private, while not expecting supporters to reveal their support in public. This leads to the irony of a public spectacle sustained by people who do not really support it. And this was public spectacle that would continue at the next meeting of the board of directors and every meeting thereafter.

CEO Succession

Political division abounds when succession is uncertain.

Although we did not have monthly board meetings—historically we had eight or nine board meetings a year—Larry Miller started calling monthly meetings. I sensed that he needed these extra meetings to sustain the spectacle, to keep the whiff of scandal in the air. He was, after all, running out of time. There were only a few months left to his two-year term as president. This particular board meeting occurred after my heart attack but before my open heart surgery. In fact at this point no one but my family and Ryan Doyle knew I was scheduled for open heart surgery. Our plan was that as soon as the surgery was completed, Ryan would release a memo to the board reporting that I had had successful bypass surgery, and that I was doing well and could take visitors. I hoped that this strategy would severely circumscribe, if not eliminate, another opening for Larry Miller to declare himself the acting CEO of the organization.

The other lesson learned from Miller's emergency meeting was that it is essential to have a successor in place when a crisis occurs. It is essential to have a clear #2 in the organization, not two or three possible successors vying with each other as many nonprofits tend to do, under the auspices of what one might call a competitive succession plan. Having a clear #2 is important because it ensures institutional continuity should something happen to the CEO and in a situation in which the crisis is a coup brought on by a combination of board ambition and staff disaffection, a #2 can counter an attempt to unseat the CEO.

But having a clear #2 means making a clear and unequivocal commitment to one person. In my case I had not yet made a clear commitment to Ryan Doyle to do whatever I could do within the scope of my power and influence to ensure that one day he would succeed me as CEO. I had not yet concluded that the competitive approach to succession might result in greater productivity initially but over time cause the kind of doubt and dissension that currently pervaded the organization. Much of that dissension had come about from the perception by some staff that Meg Michalsky was the organization's #2 and, by other staff, that Ryan Doyle was #2. My lack of leadership caused this confusion.

If I lacked the organizational experience to understand that my ambivalence about succession had caused confusion and division, I did not lack historical perspective. But perspective is only valuable if one has the wisdom to apply it. I had only to think of Winston Churchill's **History of the English-Speaking Peoples** to be reminded that political division abounds when succession is uncertain. For the peaceful transfer of power, organizations, like nations, should see succession as a single undertaking based upon loyalty and trust rather than a multiple enterprise based upon competition and envy. And succession built on cohesion rather than competition, however uncongenial it might be to the corporate world, is particularly appropriate to the higher purpose of nonprofits. But to solve the problem of succession, a CEO must act decisively and unambiguously in naming a #2, then master a majority of the board's support for a choice that the board would one day have to re-affirm. I had done neither, but to my great good fortune, Ryan Doyle had acted as if I had.

By his willingness to stand by me when others would not, Ryan Doyle had shown himself to be unwaveringly loyal and singularly trustworthy. The bond of trust between us would be born out in future years, demonstrated repeatedly by his willingness to be a buffer for me, by his willingness, as Jimmy McNally and Doug Hays liked to put it, "to take a punch" for me—which simply meant that he occasionally accepted responsibility for criticism that might otherwise have been directed at me. And I, when circumstances became too contentious for him to handle, took the heat for him.

While the Bill Hager's of the world artfully announced their loyalty to me by bullhorn, the Ryan Doyle's demonstrated theirs in selfless deeds. And while the Bill Hager's were motivated by sycophancy and self-interest, the Ryan Doyle's were transparent and self-sacrificial. How Ryan had conducted himself demonstrated to me what kind of professional he was, but more importantly, what kind of human being he was, someone in whom the admirable was the center of his soul. And as leadership criteria go, I cannot think of a more compelling criterion than an admirable soul as the basis for selecting a successor.

The Problem of Sycophancy

Well-intended sycophancy so inflates a leader's sense of himself and of his power to decide that he conflates his own willfulness with wisdom.

There would be others who would stand by me in this crisis, but none would do it as passionately, as assiduously, as fiercely, as my daughter Diane. If Ryan was a rock, Diane was Gibraltar itself. It would ultimately take the tenacity of my 5'4" firebrand of a daughter for us to win a war of wills with a personality as formidable as Meg Michalsky.

Diane came to the organization about a year after graduating from a prominent liberal arts college. She had taken a job after graduation with the marketing and communications department of a corporation but found the work uninteresting and the office politics distasteful. When the CEO of the corporation suddenly announced that the company was relocating to another city, Diane saw it as an opportunity to look for something else. While she was job-seeking, I offered her a part-time job as a gamesroom supervisor at just a little above minimum wage.

"I can't pay you what you deserve," I said to Diane, after offering her the job, "but it will put a little money in your pocket while you're looking for another position, and you'll be helping us out in the process."

"How can I refuse?" she said. "You're going to pay me the big bucks and all I have to do is play with kids."

"Yeah, right. That so-called **play** will probably be the hardest job you'll ever have."

"You sure know how to sell a job to a prospective employee."

"So you'll take it?"

"I'll take it."

"Great," I said. "Now I've got maybe the best educated gamesroom supervisor in America."

Although an occasional "knock it off!" could be heard coming from the gamesroom,

Diane handled her duties with considerable skill and aplomb and over time was able to connect with these tough, inner-city kids on a deep and fundamental level. Soon her work with these kids and the friendships she had forged supplanted any thoughts of finding another position in marketing and communications. She worked in the gamesroom for almost two years, six hours a day, thirty hours a week, in perhaps the lowest and toughest entry-level job we had, consistently performing her duties exceptionally well. She never complained and never asked for a special consideration of any kind. If there was a concern about nepotism—and one board volunteer did mention to me in passing that there were others on the board who might make my daughter's employment at the Agency an issue—it was not an issue about which I gave any considerable thought. If I had erred at all in hiring my daughter Diane, I had done so not to her advantage but to the organization's advantage.

Because the organization had more part-time than full-time positions, when a full-time position opened up it usually attracted the interest of at least some of the part-time staff. And I would, as a matter of policy, announce an opening internally before going public with it. But when I announced the availability of a full-time instructor position preparing teen dropouts for the GED—a program we were operating under the auspices of a community college without walls—none of the part-time staff applied. I knew this would not be an easy position to fill. Most of our regular agency members were in the age range of eight to thirteen, and they were much easier to work with than teens. The teens in this particular program, were all high school dropouts, and almost all of the students we had had so far had not come up through our regular core program—those kids were graduating from high school—but were referrals from residential treatment centers for addicts. So not only was this a tough clientele to deal with, but the position also required one to teach things like algebra and grammar. When no one applied, I asked Diane to take it. I needed continuity with the GED Program because it produced revenue that supported our core program for the younger kids. Diane stepped in and operated GED Program just as she had operated the gamesroom—capably, consistently, and in this case, profitably.

On my first day back after having my heart attack, and in the midst of a palace coup that was now gathering momentum, Diane, who had been teaching the basics of English grammar to eighteen-year old addicts for two years, came to me and said: "Dad, why don't you let me come back here and help you. You can get somebody else to run GED Program."

"Help me with what?"

"What else? With this fight we're in."

"I don't want you in this fight," I said. "This is my fight."

"No, Dad, this is my fight, too. What they're doing to you is **so** wrong. They're **so** out of line. You've got DiTullio sneaking in here to see Michalsky, and when he isn't doing that I'm sure he's calling her on the phone. She knew about that meeting that Miller convened with the officers. Ryan thinks she was supposed to be **in** the meeting. From where she sits she knows everything you do, everyone who calls your office, and everyone who comes here to see you. She knows when you come and go. I'm sure she knows you're having meetings with other board members. And all this stuff is getting reported to Miller and DiTullio. If we're going to beat these people, and we are going to beat them," she said, pointing a finger at me, "we have to start controlling the communications that come in and out of this administrative office."

"Michalsky already realizes things have changed with me. She no longer has the authority to schedule my appointments, and I don't I tell her who I'm meeting with or where I'm going when I leave the building, though she actually had the audacity to tell me that if I'm going to make my own schedule, I at least ought to tell her what it is."

"Dad, don't tell her anything. Move her to an upstairs office so that she has no sight line as to who comes in and out of the building, and put me back here as the receptionist and office secretary. That way I can screen every call that comes into the building."

"I think you're right about controlling the communications," I said. "But moving you in here might just give them another issue to go after me on…nepotism."

"Nepotism? I already work here; they can use it anyway. Besides, they've already thrown the kitchen sink at you. Nepotism pales by comparison. You're going to have open heart surgery in a few weeks. You're going to be out for a while. You know Miller will make another move. And this time, he'll have to deal with me."

I laughed not at what she said—which was eminently wise—but at the fire with which she said it and at the fierceness that crinkled her face. "Yeah, I guess if I had to confront you or Ryan in an alley, I'd rather it be Ryan."

Diane had persuaded me, as she and Ryan and others would from time to time persuade me about other matters, by the rigor of her reasoning and the passion of her presentation, that I ought to move Michalsky to a more isolated place in the building while I brought Diane downstairs to serve as receptionist and office manager. Only the timing of the move remained to be decided.

This exchange with Diane was another reminder to me that leaders must learn to listen carefully to those around them and be willing to act on their good counsel. The most flawed leaders are those who become too accustomed to the power of their position, which inevitably leads to two disastrous consequences: those around you will sense that what you really want from them is their unqualified support rather than their candid judgment and this well-intended sycophancy so inflates a leader's sense of himself and of his power to decide that he begins to conflate his own willfulness with wisdom.

The Problem of Perfectionism

Perfectionism taken too far tends to turn the brilliant into the banal.

Conflating willfulness with wisdom is particularly problematic for perfectionist leaders like Eileen Boyer. Though their perfectionism is noble, there is a tendency in perfectionists like Eileen to think of everyone around them as inadequate in their work ethic and their intellect, and they, therefore, begin to believe that their own positions and the decisions which follow are smarter and wiser, and when those decisions are not actually smarter and wiser, but are really the result of will over wisdom, things can, and often do, go awry. But perfectionists, aside from the burden they must bear in being smarter than everybody else—eventually driving everyone around them into a sycophantic retreat—have a tendency to push things too far and are, therefore, prone to hubris. This tendency to push things too far is fundamental to their perfectionism. Paradoxically it is their great strength but also their great weakness, because perfectionism taken too far tends to turn the brilliant into the banal. And so with standards. Where a few compelling ones might have proved invigorating, even inspiring, Eileen Boyer propagated them by the hundreds, which brought with them a bureaucratic bane of uniformity rather than originality, efficiency rather than innovation, conformity rather than candor. Standards, at least too many of them, were not at issue in my dealings with Miller, et al; rather, it was a question of too few, if any at all.

The First Principle

CEOs have to survive before they can succeed.

I decided to wait to move Michalsky upstairs until I got past the upcoming meeting of the board—my first meeting since coming back from my heart attack. Ryan and Diane and I reasoned that waiting would give us a full month before the next board meeting to gauge the nature and severity of any reaction by Miller and DiTullio. Diane came to my office to see me about an hour before the board meeting was to begin. She closed the door behind her.

"That will get reported," I said, pointing to the door as it clicked shut.

"For the last time," Diane said, referring to the plan to move Michalsky upstairs the moment the board meeting was over.

She pulled a chair from the conference table, moved it up to the front of my desk, and sat down. "How are you feeling?" she asked.

"I'm fine," I said, though I really felt fatigued and fragile, and my voice sounded faint to me.

Diane, who said, "C'mon, you have to perk up," obviously sensed that I was not myself.

"You've got to get yourself psyched up, Dad. You've got to go in there and show them that you're still in charge."

"I know," I said, but what my mind knew my body seemed to doubt. To do what my daughter wanted me to do would require an intangible of the heart to triumph over the head. Even Pascal's exhortation that the heart has its reason which reason cannot know, could not move me. What I wanted to do was lie down and sleep rather than stand up and fight.

But Diane, a fighter and a firebrand, continued her own exhortation, the last one with her fist clenched: "You can do it, Dad. You can do this."

Yes, I thought, but today I would have to do it quietly. I would have to do it as the old moralist Plutarch might have advised. Plutarch thought that the truly wise, those of strong character and moral virtue, must always be better at silence than talk. Or I could do what Sun-tzu would have advised, and make only a modest advance before quickly retreating. The strategy here would be to tire them, to make them fatigued—by modest advance and quick retreat—and thus steal their ch'i, their morale. Or in the language of the West, I would have to remember the first principle of CEO success: CEOs have to survive before they can succeed; they have to master organizational politics, which precede, and often pre-empt, organizational profits. On this particular day, too weak myself to fight, I would seek to survive to fight another day.

When the board finally convened, rather than sit at the other head of the table opposite Larry Miller, as I had been doing in recent months, I sat quietly and unobtrusively in one of the chairs against the wall. A copy of the financial statement, prepared by Meg Michalsky, was at everyone's place at the long, glass-topped conference table. The meeting agenda, which had always been prepared by me and my predecessors in consultation with the board president, was now being prepared by Larry Miller himself and brought in by him the day of the meeting. Other than the customaries—the call to order, the approval of minutes, and the finance report—neither I nor anyone else knew what was on the agenda until Larry distributed it at the start of the meeting.

But before calling the meeting to order, Larry always arbitrarily asked someone to say a prayer. I could see that most of the board volunteers were uncomfortable, even reluctant, to recite a prayer or make one up extemporaneously. A few grumbled when called upon to pray, and a few complained to me privately, but no one openly refused to do it. And prayer is what it was: Larry explicitly referred to it as a prayer rather than an invocation. I personally found the practice offensive but never openly said so. I was offended that he put people in an awkward position by asking them to say a prayer without any preparation. If he had asked me—and he did not—I would have refused. I would have said that I was offended by his presumptuous interjection of a religious practice into a business meeting of a non-sectarian institution. Few if any of us wanted to start our meeting with a prayer—a more secular invocation might have been a reasonable compromise—but none of us had the courage to tell Larry that the imposition of a religious practice was unacceptable. Our unwillingness to speak out was emblematic of the larger problem with Larry Miller: that only three of the thirty-five members of the board would ultimately be willing to challenge his other questionable behavior, much of which was yet to come, and none of them was willing to sustain that challenge over time. What support I had and what support any CEO would have when being pursued by a faction as politically motivated as Miller's was largely, and literally, silent. My only hope was that implicit in the silence was a moral purpose like that of Plutarch's.

At that particular board meeting there was one stunning development that occurred during the meeting and one inexplicable encounter that occurred afterwards. I begin with the encounter that occurred afterwards. As board members were filing out of the conference room after the meeting, I got Tommy DiTullio's attention and asked him to stay for a few minutes. We sat down across from each other in the middle of the glass-topped conference table. The door was closed and the room was exceedingly quiet except for the faint buzz of fluorescent light above us.

"Tommy, you never come around anymore."

He nodded but said nothing. His posture—he was leaning back in his chair with his head lazily cocked to the side—conveyed disinterest, maybe even indifference.

"Did I do something to offend you?"

He said nothing.

"Tommy, you and I were like brothers, like father and son, and now we don't even talk to each other. To use one of your favorite phrases, you got me puzzled. If I did something to offend you, tell me what it is, and I'll make it right."

I tried to think of how I might have offended him. That he was sensitive to the smallest slight was well known. On those occasions when I had offended him in the past, he had always accepted my apology. And as long as it had been clear that he bore no responsibility for whatever misunderstanding we might have had, he had always accepted my apology graciously and unequivocally. I kept coming back to the day when I suggested to him that Brian Billingsley succeed him as chairman of the nominating committee. Or perhaps it was, as an ex city solicitor once said to me, that Tommy had a tendency to turn on his friends. Whatever the reason for the rift between us, Tommy was either unwilling or unable to reveal it. Instead he shifted his weight, cocked his head to the other side, and sat silently, inscrutably.

"I'm completely mystified as to why you're doing this me," I said finally. "I don't see how you can line up with Larry Miller against me, especially after that performance he just put on at the board meeting."

And the performance he put on was absolutely stunning. It came at the end of an otherwise uneventful meeting, at which point he said that he had an important announcement to make. In the brief moment before he made the announcement I thought that he just might do what Greg Robertson had done and abruptly resign. What he actually did was quite the opposite. He announced that he was now retired from his position with the utility company for which he had worked since graduating from college. And to my astonishment, and to the astonishment of just about everybody in the boardroom, he added that as part of his retirement his employer "padded my wallet with sixty-six thousand dollars," leaving me, and I would later learn just about everyone else, wondering whether the money was a standard severance package or part of a calculated strategy by his employer to terminate his employment. Larry, in his closing comment, seemed to suggest an answer. He said that, although he had "retired" from his old job, he was not yet ready to retire, that he wanted everyone to know that he would now be actively looking for a new position, for a new organization that could utilize his managerial skills, and that he was seeking their assistance in his search.

For all of Larry Miller's political skills—and he had already demonstrated and would continue to demonstrate a political acumen that rivaled Tommy DiTullio's—he had handled the situation surrounding his retirement amateurishly, one could even argue, foolishly. He himself had characterized his retirement in a way that raised suspicions about the terms under which he retired. Then to say unabashedly that he wanted the board to assist him in his search seemed to suggest that he wasn't looking very far for the new position he was seeking, that in fact he was not looking any farther than the office down the hall, the one with the frosted glass window on which was painted in bold black lettering: executive director.

Unintended Consequences

When justice became a tit-for-tat scorecard for group grievances, it brought with it its own unintended consequences: a pall of injustice.

The day after Larry Miller's stunning announcement that he was looking for a job, I moved Meg Michalsky upstairs and Diane downstairs, a move which accomplished the control of the Agency's communications we wanted but brought with it unanticipated consequences. It did indeed allow me to come and go without the comings and goings being reported to Miller and DiTullio, and it did allow me to communicate by phone without the identity of callers being passed on to Miller's gang of grand inquisitors. These freedoms of movement and speech, which I had not fully appreciated until I no longer had them, were in a small way, liberating, even exhilarating. I say in a small way because the overall tone of my professional life at this point was dark and depressed. Just thinking about the investigation in which I was entangled—and I could not keep my mind concentrated on anything else—gave me a feeling of dread that I felt physically, a palpable feeling of nervous fatigue that buzzed through my body like a low current. And to live in dread for a year of one's life frays the fabric of one's humanity and does damage to the soul. It makes one slow to trust, quick to suspect. It makes one timid rather than confident and rash rather than courageous. It makes one see justice as jerry-rigged, truth as political ploy, and moderation as meager and insufficient. But however much this crisis maligned me, however much it corrupted my character, I knew like the ancients knew, that it would make me wiser than I was, that it would make me whole again, that it would bring my soul back to the equilibrium I had temporarily lost. Meanwhile, malignity reigned; it reigned from Michalsky holding court in her new hideaway of an office, and it reigned from the railings of Tommy DiTullio.

We never anticipated that moving Michalsky upstairs would actually make it easier for her to hold court with her coterie of disgruntled female staff members, all of whom had their antennae tuned to the slightest disparity of treatment, but that is exactly what happened. Even though Ryan had from his office an unobstructed site line to Michalsky's, he was rarely in his office, and Michalsky and her minions could conspire at will upstairs, while we calculated at will downstairs. Though Michalsky held court with her coterie on any number of grievances, notable among them was the idea that the men, the bro's, as they acidly referred to us, were generally treated more favorably than women. In a later memorandum to me from the personnel committee, a memo that I assumed was written by the committee's de facto counsel, Bobby Hathaway, this "point of discussion," to use the committee's term, this idea of disparate treatment, was brought to my attention under the general heading of "Discrimination Allegation."

The allegation was made by Michalsky and one other staff member and in general stated that "women feel their opinions are not valued as highly and they are not treated with the same respect that the men receive." I would have been more concerned about this supposed "point of discussion" if it had been grounded in what they thought, rather than what they felt. Their grievance was a perfect illustration to me of the absurdity of our therapeutic age in which certain of us are entitled not to have our feelings hurt. And what was meant by the suggestion that their opinions were "not valued as highly?" That their opinions were valued, but not valued highly enough? Or that they were "not treated with the same respect." Was that less respect, no respect, or disrespect?

The memo went on to state that "in particular, the women claim that certain male employees are permitted to leave work in order to attend classes, doctor's appointments and the like." In point of fact, my policy had always been flexible, for men and women alike. Many of our part-time employees were college students simultaneously working on their degrees. In fact, our agency was located on a university campus, and many of our staff attended the university while they worked for us. Had I been inflexible about staff schedules, it would have virtually eliminated the best talent pool I had for part-time staff. The real problem was that Michalsky and company were taking a literal scorecard approach to this matter, and if at any time there were more male staff than female staff whose schedules were being accorded flexibility, then their feelings would be hurt and there would be cries that the bro's were receiving favorable treatment. And how Michalsky, whose daily cigarette breaks were too numerous to count and who herself took advantage of the flexibility policy to go to the dentist and take her daughter to doctor's appointments, could be the fulcrum of discontent about supposedly disparate treatment, is hypocrisy taken to the level of farce. While the women's movement had done much to bring justice to women in the workplace, when it was taken to petty extremes, when it became a tit-for-tat scorecard for group grievances, it brought its own unintended consequence: a pall of injustice.

The Sly Fox and other Slogans

If Tommy wanted me to play the role of Sly Fox,
I would, for this one performance at least,
play it as cunningly as I could.

The other unintended consequence of moving Michalsky upstairs came right from the railings of Tommy DiTullio. For a political animal as street-smart and self-educated as Tommy, crafting slogans was an art form fit for the rough and tumble theater of local politics or, in this case, for the smaller stage of organizational politics. From the moment Meg moved upstairs, Tommy began characterizing the executive offices of the organization as The Kremlin—as a closed, controlled operation utterly lacking in transparency. Which, out of necessity, it essentially had become. With information from Meg Michalsky flowing out of the organization, it was imperative to control what little information I could, particularly information about those board volunteers whose tacit support I could count on.

The other slogan Tommy used in tandem with The Kremlin—slogans that he repeated relentlessly at board meetings and board committee meetings and virtually every public event he attended—was to refer to me as The Sly Fox, which I took as both a mendacious epithet and a high compliment. I was not then nor am I now by nature sly and cunning; I prefer to be guided by truthfulness, fairness and a respect for the rights and dignity of others. But as my old mentor Tommy had made me aware, the honorable and open-hearted almost always come to grief by the dissembling of the dishonorable. If Tommy wanted for me the role of Sly Fox, I would, for this one performance at least, play it as cunningly as I could.

Reaching a Nadir

In that brief bottomed-out moment I thought it would be best if they simply let me go.

Two weeks later, after taking a last look at the memo Ryan Doyle would release to the board announcing that I was now in the hospital recuperating from surgery, I went off to the hospital and into the uncertainty of open heart surgery. The artery that had completely closed and had caused my heart attack six weeks earlier was by-passed along with two other arteries. Perhaps because of the blood thinner I had taken to dissipate the blood clot in my heart, I started to bleed internally after surgery, and the breathing tube—though not painful per se, excruciatingly uncomfortable—was left in place in the event I had to be taken back to surgery. Because I was bleeding internally, my blood pressure dropped dramatically, and I could not, therefore, receive medication for the pain. None of this was explained to me at first, which made me so agitated that I gestured with my hands for pen and paper with which to write.

My wife Janice, while telling me that I was behaving badly, refused my request for something to write with, but my daughter Diane, who was meticulously watching over me, did not. The flurry of hastily scribbled questions that followed did not endear me to the nurses in intensive care, and later that morning my cardiologist came in and gave me a good scolding for behaving badly to my wife and to the nurses. The dressing down from the doctor, which in ordinary circumstances I would have scoffed at or completely ignored, pushed me past the point of despondency to utter despair. Here I was on the morning after major heart surgery, bleeding internally, in considerable pain because my blood pressure was too low to receive any pain medication, the tube stuck in my throat making it impossible for me to communicate, a second surgery pending, my wife mad at me, my doctor scolding me, and my entire career and personal and professional integrity in doubt.

I closed my eyes and tried to calm myself. I remembered being warned about post-operative depression, but that had yet to come. I had instead reached a nadir, the point beyond which one's humanity, one's very soul, could not go, and in that brief bottomed-out moment I thought that it would be best if they simply let me go, let me slip into the temporary mist of memory, then oblivion. But of course they would not and could not let me go. Instead they gave me a blood transfusion, which obviated the need for a second surgery, and the blood pressure went up, the morphine went in, the breathing tube came out, after which I was happily sent off by the intensive care staff to a regular room where I could scribble to Bartleby's content.

Little Things

Little minds are too much hurt by little things;
great minds see all these things too,
but are not hurt by them.
~La Rochefoucauld

As soon as I got to a regular room, Ryan came to see me to tell me about Larry Miller's latest move.

"He's really pissed off that he was never told about your surgery," Ryan said. "He wanted to know why nobody told him."

"So what did you tell him?"

"I told him he **was** told, but he complained bitterly that it was after the fact, and I said, 'What, one day after the fact?' If we had said anything sooner, he probably would have occupied your office the minute they rolled you into surgery."

Although my having surgery was not a small matter, it reminded me of Miller's preoccupation with little things, which in turn reminded me that La Rochefoucauld had once written that "little minds are too much hurt by little things; great minds see all these things too, but are not hurt by them," which in turn reminded me that volunteer leaders ought to lead by how far their intuition can see, and professional leaders (CEOs) by what their reason can touch.

"That's how Miller over-reaches, Ryan. That's how a volunteer brings down legitimate leadership to a management level. There is this constant demand for information, not policy information, not fundraising information, not the kind of information that ought to occupy a board leader, but more specific kinds of things that ought to be the purview of management. Little things. Things that you and I can quickly convey to the board at a monthly board meeting. And when this constant demand for information, for little things, is not met, he complains that he's not properly informed. This then gives him the opportunity to second-guess virtually everything we do. But that kind of information gathering, and the analysis of the information, is our job, management's job. Larry isn't pissed off because he can't properly do his job. He's pissed off that he can't do ours. He's pissed off, as you have rightly pointed out, because, for now at least, he can't do **my** job."

"For now? Don't even say that. Don't even think it."

"Don't even think what?" Diane said as she walked into my hospital room.

"That Miller and company could possibly pull off this coup," I said.

If there was such a thing as an evil eye, Diane had it, momentarily at least, riveted on Ryan. Then turning to me with a more benign look of displeasure, she said, "I thought we agreed no shop talk today, that you needed your rest."

"Yeah, you need your rest. I'll see you tomorrow," Ryan said, and he was gone.

"You scared him off," I said to Diane.

"Yeah, Ryan, the big tough guy. He's literally two of me, and he's afraid of me."

"He's not the only one."

"You don't have to be," she said. "You're my dad. Now Miller, DiTullio, Michalsky, and the rest of that crowd? That's another matter. That's another day. Right now, it's rest and sleep."

A Melancholy Mood

Living the life of the stoic meant keeping death in the foreground so as to put the good life, the life of virtue, in high relief.

Two days later they pulled tubes the size of garden hoses out of my mid-section and sent me home with a bloated belly and a chest that felt like slabs of frozen fish. It would take two years for my thinning head of hair to come back, for the frozen fish to thaw, for my frail frame to fill in again. But at least at home, under the tough love of the love of my life, my wife Janice, whose kindness to me did not extend to tolerating self-pity, I made steady progress.

It was spring. The sun, which had been

vacationing elsewhere on the planet, returned in time to melt away the last sooty mounds of snow. So the day after I came home I started to walk up and down the block, once a day at first, then twice, then a little farther each time. I could think clearly while I walked, think in a way that was concentrated, reflective, and I noticed, as my old college teacher and mentor Bob Terry had said of his own heart surgery, that I could think clearly but not as quickly as I once could. I had, in the ball-playing vernacular of my youth, lost a step. But in time the intellectual step that I lost, by the grace of what power I do not know, would come fully back to me, and on the far side of middle age I would eventually feel, perhaps because my life experiences were now long enough to reveal some truths to me and perhaps because my reading and reflecting over the years had now coalesced into some small bank of wisdom, that my mind was better than it had ever been, and better than it would ever be again. But my old mentor was also right about the darkness that would soon descend, a melancholy that made me wonder once again whether it was worth fighting the "little minds" that had lined up against me.

Diane, who was quiet by nature but fiery

and formidable in a fight, said to me one afternoon as she brought me my mail and some checks to sign, "Don't even think about packing it in, Dad. There's no way in hell we're packing it in. And let that crowd win? No way in hell."

But I was in somber rather than fighting form. I was in a melancholy mood but I knew that my daughter Diane was right. It was fighting in the face of adversity that was really required. This reminded of a stanza of a poem that I had memorized long ago. "'And O if Thou art truly in the heavens, accept my gratitude for all Thy gifts and I shall try to fight the good fight. Amen."

"Now **that** I like," she said. "Fighting the good fight. So who is that from? Some war poet? Maybe some 19th century romantic?"

I told her it was from a poem written in 1946 by John Gunther, Jr., about a year before he died of brain cancer. I explained that Gunther, who was seventeen when he died, was an exceptionally bright and talented young man who otherwise was headed to Harvard. The senior Gunther, his father John, wrote a beautifully poignant memoir about his son called **Death Be Not Proud**, which I noted was widely read by school children in the 1950s and 1960s. I first read it as a freshman in high school and had re-read it recently.

"Well, we'll fight the good fight as if this were a fight to the death," Diane said, "even though we're going to leave death and dying out of this. We've got to keep things on a positive plane, on getting better, getting stronger, on **living**, Dad, not dying."

I could see that my daughter, who was a melancholy soul herself, was trying mightily to lift me up from a melancholic mood, though with me melancholy was more of an intellectual choice than a matter of temperament, a choice that in my youth I was simply too young to make, but now, well into middle age, I was by experience and by education prepared to consider living the life of the Stoic, the life of duty and virtue and civic engagement. Living the life of the Stoic meant keeping death in the foreground so as to put the good life, the life of virtue, in high relief. But keeping death in the foreground was not always easy to do. As one of the great students of human nature, La Rochefoucauld, deftly observed, "Neither the sun nor death can be looked at steadily." Still, I was determined, however bright the glare, to look steadily at life's larger meaning, even if it meant retreating to the only safe citadel, to the only place I could truly control, my mind. And once there, with the advice of the great Epictetus in mind, I reminded myself that my adversaries could ruin my reputation and wreck my career but they could not hurt me unless my own opinion concurred with their actions.

Audit as Investigation

For Miller and company the audit was no longer a disinterested financial exercise but an investigation into potential improprieties.

There was no retreating with my daughter Diane. She was a warrior for whom fighting the good fight was the only honorable position to take when attacked. And the latest line of attack, she believed, would be directed at our audit.

"Why do you think so?"

"Because Michalsky has been taking her smoke breaks with the guy our auditors have sent out to do the field work."

"Same guy we had last year?"

"Same guy," Diane said. "Tom. He looks

like he's about seventeen. And he and Michalsky don't just stand outside the building. They go across the street and stand inside the first level of the parking garage. I saw them there yesterday, after work, and it looked like they were having a pretty spirited conversation, maybe even arguing. Something's up."

The "something's up" was this: Michalsky was telling Miller and company that Tom, the auditor, had wanted to go before the board last year to report some improprieties but I had prevented him from doing so. The supposed improprieties involved one consultant who was not issued a 1099 (Michalsky claimed, falsely, that I instructed her not to issue it), and the claim, by Michalsky apparently, that far too much of our budget was being spent on staff rather than program. Michalsky , as it was later revealed to me by Brian Billingsley, even said as an aside that all Diane does is open the mail and answer the phone, implying that Diane's position was administrative overhead that the organization could do without.

Actually the auditors had every opportunity to appear before the board on the audit year to which Michalsky referred and on every other year. The extent of the auditors' appearance before the board was and has always been a decision made by the finance committee. Minimally, the auditors, including the firm's partner who was overseeing the audit, appeared before the finance committee, and, in some years, at the finance committee's discretion, before the full board. And if the auditors did not appear before the full board, the board treasurer would present the audit to the board and would provide copies of the audit for the board's review. I had absolutely no control over the auditors' access to the board, nor did I have any influence over what the auditors reported to the board.

As to the claim that we were spending a disproportionate amount of our budget on administration, there has not been a year since I have been the CEO in which we did not perform above the national average in the ratio between program and administrative expenditures. In recent years, our program expenditures, as a percentage of expenses determined independently by our auditors, have been in a range of 82 to 85 per cent, well above the national average of approximately 65 per cent.

Failing to convince others on the board that I was interfering with the work of the auditors and redirecting program resources into an unnecessarily inflated administration, Miller and company tried to redefine the nature of the audit itself. For them the audit was no longer a disinterested financial exercise but an investigation into potential improprieties. I realized this when I received a letter from Larry Miller stating that "At the next regularly scheduled meeting of the Executive Board, I will propose that it will be beneficial for the organization to commission a full audit of its financial records for the previous fiscal year. It is my understanding that the accountants currently do a review. In order to avoid unnecessary effort or duplication of effort, I ask that you contact the organization's accountants and ask them how they suggest that we should proceed."

Miller's letter was extraordinary in its form and in its argument. Its form was what I would characterize as legal, with Miller's name and address centered at the top, and a signature line bottom right under which Miller's name was typewritten and on which he had signed his name. He had never before sent me a formal letter like this, so I first assumed it had been prepared by a lawyer, probably by Bobby Hathaway. The argument contained in the letter, that our auditors were currently conducting a review rather than a full audit, was even more striking. As long as I had been CEO of the organization, it had been my understanding that we had never engaged an auditor to conduct anything but a full audit, a distinction a lawyer of Bobby Hathaway's caliber would have known. I then wondered if perhaps Tommy DiTullio, who had worked with city solicitors over the years on claims made against the city, had advised his new protégé to make his letter look more legally persuasive. Tommy had apparently forgotten that I was partly his creation, that I was The Sly Fox and, therefore, wisely if not cunningly called the lead auditor to confirm what I suspected to be true.

Rick Noonan, the partner at the auditing firm with whom our finance committee had made the audit engagement and who was providing overall supervision to Tom, the field auditor, was the most loquacious accountant I had ever met, which was part of his charm as a person, but also professionally bright and eminently reasonable. I called Rick as soon as I got Larry Miller's letter, and read it to him over the phone.

"Where did he get the idea we were only

doing a review?" Rick said.

"I don't know, but I have to tell you there have been some allegations, false allegations I should say, made against me, one of them of a financial nature."

"Well, first of all, for an organization smaller than yours, a review might be appropriate, but what we're doing for your organization is a full audit. As for these supposed allegations, that's not part of our audit."

"So there is no higher level of audit beyond what you're doing for us?"

"No, there isn't," Rick said. "What you're getting is a full audit."

"So the allegation that's been made against me, that doesn't automatically become a part of this audit? The reason I say that is, Larry and others believe that that's what the audit ought to do: investigate any financial allegations."

"Michael, an audit is not an investigation, and to turn it into one would seriously compromise the ethical standards for which we as professional accountants are accountable."

"I think Tom is getting drawn into this effort by Meg Michalsky, to turn the audit into some kind of investigation."

"He better not be," Rick Noonan said. "And if he is, that will end today."

Reshuffling the Board

These are the new committee assignments for the board.

What would not end was the attempt to topple me. That effort and my effort to counter it would continue on and off stage for as long as Larry Miller could control the agenda of the board. Actually the coup to topple me would continue for as long as Larry held the powers of the presidency, powers which he was now beginning to understand more fully and exploit more effectively. The next public staging of this political play would be at the upcoming board meeting, the first board meeting in my entire tenure as CEO that, because of my recuperation, I could not attend. I asked Patrick McSweeney to come to town to stand in for me. Virtually all of the members of the board knew Patrick because he had on two previous occasions facilitated planning processes for us, one for a capital campaign and the other for a strategic plan. My thinking was that Patrick's presence might constrain Miller and company from making any bold moves in my absence, that having an outsider present might calm matters somewhat. Larry Miller, oddly enough, did not need to be constrained, because at the last moment he called and said he was having car problems and would not be able to make the meeting. For someone who insisted on calling a meeting every month, a grind-it-out strategy that was wearing down the middle majority of independents still loyal to me, Larry Miller missing a board meeting, especially a meeting at which he had a reasonable expectation I would not attend, was inexplicable to me. Was this a signal that his political will was waning? He would answer this question unequivocally at the next board meeting by making his boldest move yet.

Like every other board meeting during the last year of the Miller regime, a notice of the meeting went out to the board, which I then followed with a phone call to every board member whom I considered favorable to me and every other fair-minded soul whom I thought would give me the benefit of the doubt. I wanted to make sure that I had enough votes at any board meeting to prevent Miller from making a move to dismiss me. What I learned from my earlier one-on-one meetings with board volunteers and my phone calls imploring them to attend the next meeting was that most of them were suffering from a combination of volunteer fatigue and of the kind of anxiety that comes from constant conflict. The other thing I learned was that the small faction that Miller and DiTullio started with had grown to a number close to a simple majority. This growth in their numbers was due largely to Tommy's charm and the Boss-Tweed-like politics of plying people with prosciutto and red wine.

As that fateful board meeting opened with a prayer and a call to order, I found myself day-dreaming, a dreamy but pensive practice I had carried with me from my boyhood days in grade school, when, with some regularity, I was reprimanded by the good Sisters of Saint Joseph for not paying attention in class. My daydreaming now made me wonder if perhaps the metaphorical pound of flesh my adversaries had already exacted might be enough for them to forgo any further efforts to topple me. I soon found out, as Larry Miller passed out what I first thought was the meeting agenda, that they were not forgoing further efforts to topple me, but were in fact re-doubling their efforts. This redoubling of effort took the form of a radical reshuffling of all of the board committees, about which, Larry Miller, who sat stone-facedly across from me at the other end of the long glass-topped conference table, simply said, "These are the new committee assignments for the board."

An equally stony silence followed as we all studied the document. I immediately noticed that the two committees that universally defined the political dynamic of a non-profit institution, nominating and personnel, were now made up almost exclusively of Miller's core group of partisans. Tommy DiTullio of course remained nominating chairman. An old guard board member, Curt Schroeder, replaced Brian Billingsley as the chairman of the personnel committee. Ed Bolden, Larry's old coach and a connoisseur of Tommy's homemade red; Connie Santone, the young marketing maven with close ties to Tommy; and Bobby Hathaway—they had been appointed to both nominating and personnel. Many of my most loyal supporters found themselves assigned to the building committee, reminding me of the laugh Tommy and I once shared when we relegated some of Peter Matthew's supporters to the dead-end building committee. The tactics I taught Tommy were now being used against me.

There was a buzz in the room now, of natural groupings talking, of sidebar conversations, over which I asked Larry Miller why, with just a few months left to his presidency, he made a major overhaul of board committee assignments.

"Because it's within the scope of my authority to do so," he said.

"That's not what I asked," I said all the way from the other head of the long table, the one without the wooden mantle behind it. "I asked why you did it."

"Like I said, it's within my power as president to assign people to committees, and these are the new assignments."

"Did you survey the board?" I said. "Did you at least ask people what committee they wanted to serve on?"

"Nobody asked me," said Danny Ackerman in a loud irritated tone. Danny Ackerman was old guard and old school. He had come to the organization as a kid. He was a retired labor leader who had little use for Larry Miller and even less for Tommy DiTullio.

"Nobody asked me either," said Nick De-

Meo, an alumnus and retired small business owner.

The buzz of astonishment in the room seemingly went up a decibel to a full grumble of discontent.

Then Danny Ackerman hit the table. "Yeah, what the hell's going on here? You serve on a committee, you come to every meeting, you do what needs to be done, and this is the thanks you get?"

Wisely, Larry Miller answered these questions with a Delphic silence.

I took a more specific line of attack. "How is that Brian Billingsley is not even on the personnel committee? He's the former chairman, which would at least provide some continuity, and he is the only labor attorney on the board. He is the only real expert we have."

"No," Larry said, "Bobby (Hathaway) also practices labor law."

"Since when," I said. "Bobby is a corporate attorney."

Bobby Hathaway, flashing that famous boyish but overconfident grin, said, "I have practiced some labor law."

"I still think Brian should be on the personnel committee," I said, to which Danny Ackerman hit his fist to the table again and said, "I second that."

"And Nick DeMeo and Danny Ackerman should be put back on the nominating committee," I said.

Larry's stone face now showed cracks of confusion and uncertainty. He hesitated, but instead of looking to his counsel, Bobby Hathaway, he turned to Tommy DiTullio, who motioned with his forefinger for Larry to go on to the next item on the agenda.

"I'd like to continue with our agenda…" Larry started to say when he was interrupted by Danny Ackerman. "There's a motion on the floor," Danny said, raising his voice.

"Nobody made a motion," Tommy DiTullio mumbled inaudibly.

Larry then waved his hand dismissively at Tommy, and said as he started to write on his copy of the board committee assignments: "Okay, but this is the last change I'm making. I'm putting Brian Billingsley on personnel and Nick DeMeo on nominating. That's it. Let's move on."

Bigger Boards are Better

...they make it more difficult for a faction like Miller's to carry off a coup against the CEO.

After the meeting I went directly to my office and pulled out my copy of the constitution and by-laws. I wanted to double check on whether the by-laws clearly established a maximum number of board volunteers for membership on the board. I knew from colleagues in the Youth Association field and from friends of mine who were CEOs of local organizations that some of them had by-laws which allowed for an unlimited number of board volunteers. Bigger boards are better than smaller boards because they extend the fundraising reach of the organization and they make it more difficult for a faction like Miller's to carry off a coup against the CEO. If our board had been half the size, a total of eighteen instead of its current thirty-six, Miller and DiTullio might have been able to secure the few swing votes they needed to topple me.

But unlike virtually all of the nonprofit CEOs I knew, I had, thanks to the political acumen of my mentor, Patrick McSweeney, political protection over which Miller's and DiTullio's near majority could not prevail: the policy written into the by-laws that required a super-majority vote to terminate the CEO. When a board moves against a CEO with unanimity, a super-majority requirement to terminate is superfluous, but when the board is more evenly divided, and there are some moderates and independents in play politically, a super-majority requirement is decisive. But even the super-majority requirement to terminate the CEO would not be insurmountable to a politically motivated board president, one whose cronies not only controlled the nominating committee but also had the latitude to bring on as many board members as they thought politically necessary. Luckily Larry Miller and company did not have that political latitude.

Our by-laws capped the number of people who could serve on the board at forty, and it also required board volunteers to be county residents. So there was no possibility of bringing ringers in from out of town, nor was there much latitude to pack the board with only four slots available—though four new volunteers favorable to Miller and DiTullio, by my count, would have given them simple majority support to run me and Ryan and Diane out of the organization. Not yet enough for them to prevail, but with so many of my supporters fatigued from the fight, from the war of attrition being waged by Miller and DiTullio, I had very serious doubts as to whether I could win a war waged so resolutely, so ambitiously, so cunningly, against me. If I had any doubts about what Miller and DiTullio might do now that they controlled the personnel committee, they were clarified by a five-page memorandum I received from Bobby Hathawy entitled "Talking Points."

Talking Points

They should not be read as accusations but instead interpreted as opportunities to disclose the facts…

"These 'talking points' are designed to elicit a free exchange of information regarding various issues. They should not be read as accusations but instead interpreted as opportunities to disclose the facts relevant to each issue. The points have been drafted as specifically as reasonably possible, but should not be read to exclude responses that are relevant although not necessarily responsive to any talking point.

"Many of these points are reflective of

concerns of Larry Miller and other members of the Board of Directors. Others reflect allegations made by former employees. Attached hereto are letters and other written statements from these former employees. It is anticipated that the relationship between the organization and these former employees may be pertinent to evaluating their allegations.

"The contents of this memo and all attachments should be kept strictly confidential. No current staff members should be allowed to review the documents or otherwise be informed of their content. It is acknowledged that this memo and attachments may necessarily be shared with a discreet number of board members for the purposes of insuring a full and fair response. Any board members with whom these documents are shared should be advised of the importance of keeping these documents and their contents confidential."

Larry Miller, through his legal counsel, Bobby Hathaway, was directing me to keep confidential what everybody in the organization, and many outside of it, already knew: that Miller and company were open to any allegation anyone would like to make against me, and to a lesser extent against

Ryan and Diane, no matter how reckless the rumor, no matter how unsupportable the assertion. It was nice to know that these allegations were not really allegations. They were "talking points." They were "opportunities to disclose the facts" and encourage "a free exchange of information." They were simply the "concerns of Larry Miller and other members of the Board of Directors." And even though some of the "concerns" were implicitly and explicitly directed at Ryan and Diane, no "current staff members" were allowed to know about the document or its contents. Their idea of a free exchange of information was positively Orwellian. Freedom on their terms was not really freedom at all, but its opposite: constraint. The supposed desire for a fair response was inherently unfair in that I could not use this information to defend myself adequately or to help Ryan and Diane defend themselves against an investigation that had degenerated into a rumor-driven witch hunt. Of course the talking points were not talking points at all. They were allegations posed as questions. Or they were simply directives for me to provide them with certain kinds of information. The overall implication of this memorandum was that they were fishing for anything they could find, and they had cast their net wide enough to catch the biggest rumors and the smallest innuendos. And virtually all of the catch that follows had the stink of dead fish.

The Committee-Driven Approach to Governance

...drives an organization to the quotidian rather than the grand, to the margins rather than the center, to make-work rather than real work, to strategic planning rather than strategic thinking.

"How frequently do standing committees hold formal meetings? Please set forth the dates in the last two years when each of the standing committees has held a formal meeting. If any committee has not held a formal meeting in the last year, please explain why and offer suggestions as to how we can ensure more frequent and meaningful committee meetings."

Since I had yet to formulate fully my counter-strategy to their investigation, I simply complied with their request for information, but added the dates of the ad hoc committees. Two of the ad hoc committees were organized around fundraising events, and these committees met much more frequently than all standing committees except finance. As I think about it now, I should have refused to provide this information to Bobby Hathaway. I should have told him I would be happy to debate these issues before the full board, at which time I would provide information about the recent activity of all committees. I knew that the personnel committee would ultimately be accountable to the full board. I also knew that I still had majority support on the board. What was implied in this request for information was that I had been running the organization without committee, or more precisely, board oversight. The reality is that the finance committee was meeting monthly, the fundraising committees bi-monthly, and other standing committees, like personnel and nominating, were meeting on an as needed basis, two times a year on average. Committees in general have an important but limited role to play in the professional life of a non-profit leader. Only finance, personnel (or human resources) and nominating (or board development) are essential committees. Others might add marketing and communications to the list of essential committees.

When a committee has nothing to discuss,

no policy issue to develop or revisit, it should not convene. Miller and company wanted committees to meet whether they had a reason to meet or not. Even our national organization, through its Standards of Organizational Effectiveness and through its workshops offered at conferences, advocated for a committee-driven approach to governance, and by extension, to management. The committee-driven approach calls for every committee, standing or ad hoc, to establish goals and objectives of its own, which would be, in theory at least, consistent with the mission, vision and strategic direction of the organization.

In practice, the committee-driven approach to governance drives an organization to the quotidian rather than the grand, to the margins rather than the center, to make-work rather than real work, to strategic planning rather than strategic thinking. Committees, if given enough encouragement, will go off in directions unintended and unnecessary, and in the process attenuate CEOs' capacity to lead by bogging them down in meetings and projects of dubious value. Committees typically extend their reach beyond governance into management, beyond policy into procedure, and ultimately undermine the role of the full board as the true policy-maker and governing entity. That is why CEOs would be wise to start all policy discussions with the full board, even if the initial discussion is unwieldy and inchoate, before assigning it to a committee. Once a committee studies a policy issue and makes a recommendation to the full board, the most likely result is that the committee recommendation becomes, after minimal discussion and debate, a fait d'accompli. By getting everyone on the board of directors engaged at the beginning of the policy-making process, the full board, not the factional will of particular committees, can maintain its position as the true governing entity of the organization, and the CEO can take the time and can seize the strategic latitude to perform a CEO's first function: to lead.

More Talking Points, More Explanations

As the weeks went by…I came to realize the folly of fighting innuendo and ill will with rational argument.

But with Larry Miller's eleventh hour committee reorganization, we were now down to a committee composition even more uncomplicated than my own. I will call it the crony committee, because Miller's cronies now constituted both the personnel and the nominating committees, with one exception on each committee. Which brings me back to Bobby Hathaway's memorandum on behalf of the crony committee (personnel version) and its investigation, back to the rarified world of talking points.

"Is it true that the Executive Director has been using an agency-leased van for matters not directly related to the operations of the agency?"

Not in the way Meg Michalsky had characterized it to the committee. She contended that the vehicle was essentially used for my personal purposes. Whether this distinction mattered or not, there were members of the committee, particularly Tommy DiTullio, who had already established that I used the vehicle to transport them.

"Is it true that staff members have, while on organization time, painted the executive director's house?"

Michalsky fingered two staff whom she wanted to believe painted my house. They were both called before the committee, and both were unequivocal in stating that they had not at any time under any circumstances done any work at my house.

"Presumably, the executive director and staff members personally incur expenses that are reimbursed by the organization. Please describe how these expenses are documented."

Hathaway and the committee knew quite well how travel and business expenses were documented. The real issue was whether I had expensed some meals to the organization account that were not business related. They would have a surprise for me, and I for them, when I finally appeared before the personnel committee for my grilling by Miller's grand inquisitor and legal footman, Bobby Hathaway.

"Is it a policy or has it been the policy of the agency that staff members are not permitted to speak with members of the Board of Directors? If so, please explain the rationale for this policy."

"Is it the policy or has it been the policy of the organization that some staff members are not permitted to speak to other staff members? If so, please provide the details of the policy by detailing which staff members are not permitted to speak to other staff members and why.

"Is it the policy or has it been the policy of the organization that only certain staff members are permitted to answer the telephone? If so, please list those employees who are not permitted to answer the telephone. Also, please describe the rationale for prohibiting these employees from answering the telephone."

All of these communications issues were little more than malicious mischief prompted by Meg Michalsky.

"Is it true that the executive director locks his door during business hours and permits no one to enter without the approval of his assistant? If so, please describe the rationale for this conduct."

I did close my door occasionally, as any CEO or executive might, but it was never locked, and I only closed it when Ryan and Diane and I were discussing strategy related to the ever expanding list of talking points.

"Please comment generally on the status of communications between the executive director and Larry Miller. Specifically, but not exclusively, address the following: A U.S. Senator was scheduled to be the guest speaker at the annual fundraising dinner, but the Senator was unable to attend. Larry Miller was not advised of the Senator's absence until he arrived at the dinner. This information came not from the executive director but from another board member. Needless to say, Larry was upset that he was had not been informed earlier."

I found out when Larry did—when I walked into the hotel ballroom that night.

"Does the organization have a policy with regard to the use of offensive racial, ethnic or sexual statements by staff members? If so, please describe the policy. Also, please describe how the policy is enforced."

My response was: I don't make policy; you do.

"Has the executive director or any staff member ever referred to Larry Miller as a 'dumb stupid nigger' or used any other offensive racial statement in connection with Larry Miller, any board member or youth member?"

I would not dignify that one with a response.

"Are you satisfied with the racial, ethnic and sexual makeup of the current board of directors or do you believe that the organization should endeavor to increase the representation of women and racial and ethnic minorities? Are there efforts currently underway to increase the representation of women and racial or ethnic minorities on the board of directors? If so, please describe these efforts."

My own answer to this was that fairness should always prevail and, therefore, no one should be kept off the board because of their gender or race or ethnicity. The board president was, after all, African American, and I had played a pivotal role in positioning him to assume the presidency of the organization. But I also knew it was never wise to recruit people to the board on the basis of their gender or race. That kind of identity politics would ultimately be a bane on the organization. It would ultimately make room for the kind of racial and gender mischief in which we were now embroiled. Bringing identity politics to the boardroom would ultimately diminish the stature and effectiveness of a board built upon one fundamental idea: that the impact a board volunteer can have on the organization, regardless of gender or age or race or any other political category, trumps all other considerations.

"Do you believe a full audit for this past fiscal year is in the best interests of the organization? Why or why not?"

What I believed was that a lawyer of Bobby Hathaway's caliber should have made sure he understood the difference between a review and an audit, and more importantly he should have understood that an audit could not be turned into a financial witch hunt at the behest of Machiavellians like Miller and Michalsky and DiTullio.

"It is believed that you have recently demoted or repositioned one or more long time organization employees and promoted your daughter to a position formerly held by another employee. If true, please explain the rationale for these decisions. Also, do you feel that this action has resulted in employee morale problems and, if so, what do you think should be done about those morale problems?"

Actually, I promoted Meg Michalsky and demoted my daughter Diane. And to suggest that these staff moves were responsible for a morale problem among the staff was so laughable as to be patently ridiculous. Staff morale had long been poisoned by the anti-Doyle, anti-male machinations of Meg Michalsky. That is why I could not let Michalsky control the official communications of the company. She already controlled the unofficial communications of the company.

Then there was the matter of Michalsky making it known to Ryan Doyle and to others on the staff that she could do my job better than I, a boast that made me wonder whether this bookkeeper with a high school diploma was naïve enough to believe that the board would pick her to succeed me. Perhaps it was not naivete at all. Perhaps it was self interest blinded by ambition or simply a self incapable of making a wise and proper estimate of itself and its true nature. But even if she thought she could do my job, she had to know that her qualifications were monumentally inadequate. She also had to know that she could never be my successor as long as Larry Miller was board president and was himself waiting in the wings.

As the weeks went by, and talking points appeared and disappeared at the arbitrary will of arbiters like Larry Miller and Bobby Hathaway, I came to realize the folly of fighting innuendo and ill will with rational argument. I realized that the attempts to explain myself, the attempts to counter talking points point for point, were the equivalent of a rational person trying to persuade an irrational person to think and act rationally.

My attempts to explain myself, which Patrick McSweeney aptly characterized as a pissing contest that I could not win, had the effect of reducing rationality to its opposite: irrationality.

Just Don't Call it a Witch Hunt

But once you start looking into it, there will be fair-minded people who will begin to believe it and people who are not fair-minded who will exploit it.

In a fair fight, especially one in which the power to control an institution is not at stake, logical argument can be compelling. But in a coup—and Patrick McSweeney had on a number of occasions compared my circumstances to a coup—logic is of little value. I realized then that to counter a coup I would have to turn to the kind of manipulative marketing I otherwise would have preferred to avoid. I realized I needed a slogan to discredit those who were working furiously to discredit me. One slogan probably would have been sufficient, but I decided on two: Larry's looking for a job (my job, of course), and instead of referring to the investigation as an investigation, I referred to it, over and over again to anyone who would listen, as a witch hunt. Over time—and the witch hunt went on for weeks, months really—the two slogans conduced to: Larry Miller launched this witch hunt so he could take Michael Palermo's job.

I would wonder for a long time whether these slogans were unethical. I would wonder how much truth they actually contained. Larry Miller himself said he was looking for a job, but would he countenance a coup and encourage it to continue for weeks and months so he could step into my position? My guess is that he had not initiated it—that it had actually been initiated by staff—but once the opportunity to topple me presented itself, he sanctimoniously seized it. As for the investigation taking on the temper of a witch hunt, that seemed, to me at least, undeniable. All that fabrication and falsity could not sustain itself without ulterior or political motives.

My marketing strategy worked. At the next meeting of the board, Larry Miller launched into a vigorous denial of the idea that he was in any way interested in my job. He seemed genuinely irritated by the implications of such a suggestion. If he had been testifying in court and I had been one of the jurors, I would have found his testimony believable. I don't doubt that his friends and supporters on the board found him believable. But the rest of the board, the majority—as it was expressed to me in sidebar conversations during and after the board meeting, and in phone conversations that followed the meeting—did not find Larry's protestation believable. As one board member said to me, "It's pretty obvious. He wants your job."

What was motivating Larry Miller was not at all obvious to me. As Henry James had long ago observed, no one can know with finality what is in any human heart. There was always the possibility that he saw himself as doing his civic duty. Even Brian Billingsley, a lawyer of unimpeachable integrity, a man who would later become a deacon in his church, made it clear to me that the board had an obligation to investigate these allegations.

"So anyone can make any allegation against me, no matter how preposterous, no matter how unsubstantiated," I said to Brian Billingsley one day after he had called me to tell me about the personnel committee's most recent meeting, "and the committee is obligated to investigate it?"

"I wouldn't say **that**."

"But someone can say that Ryan Doyle and I are going around town using racial epithets even if that someone has never heard us say any such thing?"

"I didn't say it was fair," Brian said. "I simply said we had an obligation to look into it."

"Yes, but once you start looking into it, there will be fair-minded people who will begin to believe it, and people who are not fair-minded who will exploit it."

"That may be so," Brian said, "but then again, we can't just ignore it."

"But that's just it. You can and should ignore it if there's nothing to corroborate it. Reputable journalists could not publish a story like that unless they had two sources who heard me say some racial epithet about Larry Miller. Your committee is pursuing that allegation on the basis of having no one who heard me or Ryan say any such thing. And the reason you don't have anybody is that I wouldn't under any circumstances, even in the privacy of my own home, even in the privacy of my own conscience, say such a thing, and you know it."

"I agree," Brian said. "That particular allegation should have been summarily tossed out."

"But it wasn't."

"No, it wasn't"

"Which is why this whole investigation is nothing more than a witch hunt."

"I wouldn't call it a witch hunt," Brian said.

"You yourself asked me if I had my house painted recently, Brian."

"Only to help you prove that it wasn't painted by staff," he said. "That hardly establishes your claim that this investigation is nothing more than a witch hunt."

"Why should I have to prove that I didn't do something? Isn't that your burden, the committee's burden, to prove that I did?"

"I was just trying to help you dispense with that allegation before the committee started calling witnesses in an attempt to substantiate it."

"Brian, if I didn't paint my house, I can't tell you I had some painting company paint my house."

"Fine," Brian said, dismissively, irritably.

I could see that I was alienating my only ally on the committee, a man who had been kind enough and fair-minded enough to allow me to call him after every committee meeting to find out what had happened.

One Friday evening in September, near the end of the committee's investigation, Brian told me that the committee was planning to call two employees, Carl Kolenda and Jamie McDermott, to appear before them to answer questions about whether they participated in painting my house.

"Brian, what I don't understand is, on what basis are Carl Kolenda and Jamie McDermott connected to this allegation?"

"According to Meg Mihalsky, they punched in on their time cards one day, but never punched out, nor were they seen the rest of the day."

"Seen by whom?"

"Meg, of course."

"Why would she see them. She doesn't even supervise them. Ryan does."

"Well it is legitimate to ask where they were that day," Brian said. "As the executive director, you should be concerned about that, right?"

"That may well be, but I don't see what that has to do with this witch hunt."

"It may end up having nothing to do with it," Brian said, "which would compel the committee to scratch that allegation off the list."

"So these guys get hauled before the kangaroo court for no other reason than they didn't punch out on their time card, and may have, just may have, played a little hooky on a summer day when the organization was in shutdown for cleaning and repairs."

"Michael, if that's all it is, then we won't have a problem."

"Well, sorry, but I have a problem with it."

"I can tell you that Bobby Hathaway thinks it's important to watch their demeanor when they appear before the committee."

"I don't much care what Bobby Hathaway thinks."

"You might want to rethink that," Brian said. "Because Connie Santone said that, even if all the remaining allegations are true—and there are six or seven that the committee's still considering—you should not be terminated, but reprimanded, Bobby agreed with that."

"Well, since none of it is true, the whole damn thing should be shut down now, instead of hauling people in to see what their demeanor's going to be."

"I can't say that I disagree with you, Michael, but with Curt Schroeder as the chair, and Larry and Tommy, Joyce George, and Ed Bolden, they're one vote short, mine, of unanimity."

"So when do Carl Kolenda and Jamie McDermott appear before the committee?"

"Next week."

"Is that it, then?"

"Larry still wants to call some other people before the committee. Then of course you'll get your opportunity to appear before the personnel committee."

"Who else are they talking about?"

Brian named names: former employees, the field auditor from the auditing firm, and the staff member who was supposedly the source of the racial epithet allegation, Bill Hager.

"Brian, the race remark question has already been asked and answered. Bill Hager looked Larry in the eye and told him that neither Ryan nor I ever said any such thing. Maybe they just want to look at his demeanor, right? This has gone on way too long. Maybe it's time for me to get a lawyer."

"You lawyer up and they'll just be more convinced that you're guilty of these allegations"

"Then I'm going to write Curt Schroeder a letter telling him that it's time this witch hunt ended."

"Fine," Brian said. "Just don't call it a witch hunt."

When Compromise Candidates Become Committee Chairs

What I should have known from the beginning was that he was not the non-partisan unifier he was touted to be.

Curt Schroeder was a semi-retired lawyer with a Harvard law degree and a purple heart for his service in WWII. He had been appointed president of the board by acclamation to finish Greg Robertson's term. The board believed that Curt could at least preside over, if not remedy, the divisiveness that resulted from the demotion and departure of Matt Mihalak. And that is what he did: he presided over a relatively uneventful term while divisions remained dormant, only to resurface later with renewed ferocity during the Larry Miller regime. Although Curt Schroeder could be a curmudgeon, I got along with him reasonably well during his presidency. We met on a bi-weekly basis, almost always in my office, and almost always to sign checks, which required both of our signatures. While we signed checks, I would use the time to brief him about the next board meeting or any other matter about which I thought he needed to be apprised. Occasionally, I would seek his advice, but I sought it sparingly because I knew that any unresolved issue or problem would prompt him to say, "Well, let's cover our ass on that; let's call the committee together."

What I did not know about Curt Schroeder and what I should have known from the beginning was that he was not the non-partisan unifier that he was touted to be. He was actually one of the most partisan people on the board. He had been, along with Peter Matthews and Greg Robertson and others, completely enamored with Matt Mihalak. When Tommy DiTullio started undermining Matt Mihalak, Curt repudiated Mihalak with the same prickly partisanship with which he had once admired him. So when the board picked Curt as a compromise candidate for board president, we were not getting a man with a moderate sense of proportion, but a partisan whose passions were always well to one side of the spectrum or the other.

Based on my own personal observations—I had, for instance, seen Curt huddling with Tommy DiTullio—and on information that Brian Billingsley was privy to, I now knew that Curt Schroeder's animus was directed at me. Whereas critics like Connie Santone and Bobby Hathaway seemed willing to forgive whatever transgressions they thought I had committed, Curt Schroeder, like Larry Miller (who thought I was arrogant) and Tommy DiTullio (whose disloyalty was utterly incomprehensible to me) wanted his ass-covering personnel committee to terminate me. I did not hold out much hope that a letter to him pleading my case would do much good, but I knew that the writing of it would at least do my soul some good. So I sent Curt Schroeder a letter at the end of September.

Dear Curt:

It has been two months, and two board meetings have come and gone since the personnel committee convened to hear Meg Michalsky's complaints. The length of time this is taking and the devastating effect it is having on the organization are a very real concern to me and to many others in the organization. I think everyone's expectation, board and staff alike, was that this matter would be concluded judiciously and expeditiously, but unfortunately it has been neither fair nor fast, and as a result it has jeopardized our programming, our fundraising, and the safety and quality of the services we provide to the children.

The conduct of the committee is also a concern. The practice of bringing in former employees to report rumors and make allegations against other staff is a clear violation of organizational policy. These employees had ample opportunities during their employment here to have their complaints heard through the grievance process. For any one of them to say that she was told by a staff member not to bother because she would not get anywhere with her complaint, is fatuous, self-serving and flat-out false.

I have to this point cooperated with your request that I not attend these meetings, despite the fact that I am a member of the personnel committee. However, if it is the intention of the committee, as it has been rumored around the organization, to bring other staff before it, then I will insist that I attend the next meeting, as is my right as a member of the personnel committee.

This process has obviously gone awry. The situation it has created among staff is intolerable. Rumors are flying about staff salaries, staff are being threatened and intimidated, and at least one member of your committee has made public statements that are prejudicial to me and to Ryan Doyle, not to mention detrimental to the reputation and integrity of the organization.

I think it is past time that I be given, as agreed, any and all information—minutes, documents, letters, etc—that the committee has reviewed so I can respond to the rumors and innuendos that are being recklessly spread about me throughout the organization and the community. Continuing to drag this out any further will have long-term repercussions for the organization and for the children we serve.

Sincerely,

Michael Palermo, Executive Director

cc: board of directors

Who from the committee made public comments about the allegations leveled against me and Ryan Doyle? Tommy DiTullio. How did we find out? A staff member's spouse told us that Tommy talked about the allegations in detail in front of other customers at a store.

Who told former female employees not to bother to bring their complaints through the grievance process? Meg Michalsky.

Who caused a furor by releasing virtually all of the staff salaries? Meg Michalsky.

And who was attempting to intimidate staff? According to Carl Kolenda, Meg Michalsky said "that there was something going down with the board, that I better tell the truth, that I may have to submit to a polygraph, and that I should give her a call."

A New Era

I would aspire to become after three decades of professional experience and of broadening and deepening a love of the liberal arts the leader I hoped to be one day: the leader as liberal thinker.

A few days later Carl Kolenda and Jamie McDermott appeared before the personnel committee. In spite of my threat to do so, I did not attempt to attend the meeting. Much to the dismay of Miller and company, neither Carl Kolenda nor Jamie McDermott said that he painted my house. Carl Kolenda, who tended to be soft-spoken in general and respectful of those in authority in particular, was believable on the basis of his demeanor, whereas Jamie McDermot presented himself in a manner committee members considered arrogant, prompting Larry Miller to observe: "McDermott's arrogant, just like Palermo," But to borrow Brian Billingsley's phrase, their testimony to the committee scratched another allegation off the list. One matter remained for the committee to consider, and that was the appearance before them of their principal antagonist, me, the Sly Fox, the arrogant one, the purported perpetrator of racial mischief and gender bias and financial malfeasance. A date was set for mid October, a few days before the October board meeting, which would enable the personnel committee, as my letter to Curt Schroeder had requested, to make its final report and recommendation to the full board.

Although some of the committee's meetings had been held in the organization's conference room, my appearance before the committee was held at Curt Schroeder's office in an elegant conference room with a big window view of the bay below and the lake beyond. I was seated at one end of the table; Curt Schroeder at the other end. These were the same polar positions that Larry Miller and I shared for the final year of his presidency. Curt Schroeder, as it turned out, was every bit as tenacious as Tommy DiTullio and Larry Miller and Ed Bolden in insisting that they fire me from my position as the CEO of the organization. In fact, I could tell from where people sat and how they sat at the conference table whether they would vote for or against me. Brian Billingsley sat to my right, but his chair was pulled back several inches from the conference table, an indication to me that he had distanced himself from Curt and the rest of my detractors. Bobby Hathaway sat next to Brian, his elbows casually planted on the table top, smiling as always, but more benignly than overconfidently. Ed Bolden, who sat next to Bobby Hathaway, and Tommy and Larry who sat across from them, all sat quietly with their shoulders slightly stooped as if they were sitting in the pew of a church. Connie Santone and Joyce George, who were opposite each other at corners of the table, Joyce next to me and Connie next to Schroeder, both sat back in their chairs in a relaxed and open posture. Curt Schroeder opened the meeting and quickly turned it over to the committee's counsel, Bobby Hathaway, who, from that point on, was the only member of the committee to speak.

Still smiling benignly, the baby-faced Bobby asked me question after question for about a half hour. His tone, if not affable, was at least cordial, though his questions, particularly those relating to my use of an organization vehicle, a subject on which he spent a considerable amount of time, were aggressive and pointed. It seemed that he spent far too much time on the vehicle allegation, having established early on in his line of questioning that I had, at least on occasion anyway, used the vehicle for personal as well as professional purposes. And he already had the testimony of Tommy and other members of the committee that there had been some personal use of an organization vehicle. Bobby then turned his attention to the allegation that I had directed Meg Michalsky to tamper with a financial statement. The allegation turned on whether I had directed her to misrepresent the amount of membership revenue the organization had received.

"I didn't direct her to misrepresent anything," I said. "I simply told her that if membership revenue came from other sources, like the school district underwriting the cost of memberships for a program we operate in collaboration with them, then that revenue should be represented in the membership revenue line."

"So you didn't say to her, you better add some revenue to the membership line, because if the board sees this number, they're going to think that our membership has declined?"

"Why would I? I had no reason to. The original number that you referred to was well above the national average for an organization our size. I simply wanted all of the membership revenue to be reflected in one place, where it should be, on the membership revenue line of the budget."

Ed Bolden, who was seated next to Bobby, pushed a piece of paper to Bobby. It was a plain piece of paper with some handwriting on it and the larger membership revenue figure that they were questioning. Bobby pushed the paper in front of me and asked me if I had written it.

I looked down the table at Curt Schroeder who sat like a saturnine potentate and then back to Bobby and said, "I thought we agreed that copies of any material relevant to this inquiry would be given to me beforehand. But to answer the question: no, I didn't write that, it's not my handwriting, and if you'd like a sample of my handwriting, I'll be happy to provide it."

The paper looked to be in Meg's handwriting. I thought that perhaps Ed Bolden had misinterpreted what the document actually was: notes that Meg presumably made rather than instructions I had written to her.

Bobby Hathaway obviously had the same impression. "So that paper"—which he now pointed to—"does not reflect instructions that you gave to Meg Michalsky to change a financial statement?"

"No it does not."

Bobby Hathaway then pulled a copy of a credit card statement from a folder, pushed it to me, and said, "Can you tell us what this expense was for?"

"Again, this was not a document that was given to me beforehand, so I may not be able to identify it."

Bobby turned up the charm, smiling more benignly than before. "Well, just do your best."

It was an old statement, more than a year old, and there were two restaurant charges on it. I recognized one of the charges immediately: it was for a dinner that Tommy and I had had after attending a community event together. I knew then that Brian Billingsley had been right about Bobby Hathaway. Bobby did seem to be willing, tacitly at least, to recommend retaining me as the CEO of the agency. The credit card receipt confirmed it, because Bobby had just given me a hammer with which to pound the wiliest political animal of them all: Tommy DiTullio.

"Yes, I do recognize one of these charges." I looked down the table at Tommy. "Tommy, it was for that dinner you and I had after attending that reception up at the college."

"What?" Tommy said, as if he had not heard me correctly, though I suspected that his befuddled innocence was entirely feigned.

Larry Miller, who was seated next to Tommy, and who had not said a word the entire meeting, suddenly spoke up. "Let me see that," he said with an irritable air of skepticism.

I pushed the statement down to Larry, and while he and Tommy huddled over it and grumbled back and forth to each other, Bobby Hathaway turned to me and said that that concluded the committee's questions, that if I wanted to make any concluding remarks, I could, though he encouraged me to keep them short. When I declined the opportunity to comment, Bobby thanked me for appearing before the committee, as did Curt Schroeder, and I got up and walked out of the conference room and into the lobby of the law firm. I looked out at the lake as I walked through the lobby. The bright blue sky I had seen on the way in was now black and foreboding. As I walked through the glass doors of the law firm and into the hallway where the elevators were, I felt my throat tighten into a knot and a tear roll down my cheek. Even though the encounter with Curt Schroeder's committee could have been much worse than it was, the cumulative effect of everything that had happened in the last several months washed over me like the storm coming in off the lake. I suddenly felt a deep sense of sadness, the kind of grief one feels at the loss of a loved one. I stepped into the elevator to go down to the ground floor. I was crying now, and I realized that I had only cried one other time in my adult life, and that was when my father died ten years ago. I felt a strange sense of self-consciousness and shame, which for a long time led me to withdraw from community life.

A few days later the full board met to hear the recommendation of the personnel committee. Like every other board meeting during Larry Miller's tenure, I called everyone whom I thought would be favorable to me, and this time, perhaps out of curiosity as well as support, everyone came, as did my detractors, led this time not by Bobby Hathaway or Curt Schroeder or Larry Miller, but by Ed Bolden, who was neither an officer of the board nor the chair of the personnel committee. Ed Bolden, who had been Larry Miller's college coach and who at one time wanted to date Meg Michalsky, did have a deep personal animus toward me, the source of which seemed to come from my characterization of Larry Miller as an unprincipled opportunist.

I walked into the boardroom just before the meeting began and took a seat on the side of the room. I expected to be asked to leave, but shortly after I sat down Larry Miller called the meeting to order and introduced Ed Bolden to make the report for the personnel committee. I soon realized why Ed was asked (perhaps he volunteered) to make the report, because he may have been the only one on the committee unapologetic enough to defend an investigation that accomplished next to nothing—except to deepen divisions that had lain latent in the organization for years.

Ed's report concentrated on two broad themes: one theme was to deny that the investigation was a witch hunt (my marketing strategy had worked); the other theme was, just because the committee only recommended I be reprimanded for inappropriate use of a Agency vehicle, that did not mean I was not guilty of the other charges. It simply meant that they could not prove the other charges. So, to follow Ed's tortured logic, and the logic of Larry and Tommy, both of whom mumbled "yeah" in support of Ed's idiotic and ill-tempered claim, I may well have been guilty of any or all of the allegations leveled against me.

After the motion was made and seconded, and the board voted unanimously to reprimand me for personal use of an agency vehicle, I walked out of the boardroom and into my office which had served as little more than a war room for over a year. Waiting for me there with equal parts of hope and of apprehension were the two people most responsible for my ability to beat back the political machinations of Miller and company: my daughter Diane, whose tenacity and attention to detail made her formidable in a fight, and Ryan, whose steadfastness and loyalty made me believe that this was a war worth winning.

Shortly after that, Larry Miller's turbulent term as board president came to an end, as did

Meg Michalsky's tenure as finance director and mischief-maker. Larry had presided at his last board meeting; all that remained was the official changing-of-the-guard at our upcoming annual meeting. So with a new board president about to begin his term, a young turk who owned and operated a construction company, and who, because of his father's friendship with Tommy DiTullio, had distanced himself from the political fight that had paralyzed the organization for more than a year, I moved quickly to make the changes I should have made at the beginning of my tenure as CEO of the organization.

I met with my soon-to-be board president Denny Maloney and presented him with two lists: the first list had the names of all the board members whose terms I did not want renewed at the annual meeting. Larry Miller and Tommy DiTullio topped a list that included Ed Bolden, Bobby Hathaway, Connie Santone, Maria DiSanto, Curt Schroeder, and a few others.

"I want all of them to receive a nice letter from you, Denny, thanking them for their years of service and the many contributions they've made on behalf of the kids, and explaining to them that we'll be recognizing them at the annual meeting. We'll have a nice plaque made for each of them, whether they come to the meeting or not."

"I like that," he said. "That's good. It has to be done. But I want to suggest one change to you. Let's not remove Tommy from the board. Without Larry and the rest of them, Tommy won't be able to hurt us. And if Tommy gets out of line, and I doubt that he will, I'll take care of him. Okay?"

"Yeah, as long as he doesn't chair any committees, particularly nominating or personnel," I said as I placed in front of Denny my second list: the new committee assignments I wanted.

After looking over the list, Denny said: "This is fine, Michael, but let's put Tommy in there."

"Okay, how about the building committee?"

Denny laughed. "No, we can't do that to Tommy. We have to show him some respect. Why don't we put him on the nominating committee?"

"Nominating?"

Denny glanced down at the committee list, then looked up at me and said, "The rest of the committee, they're your people, right? They'll vote with you, right? Then Tommy can't hurt us."

"Done," I said, and with that, a new era had begun, one in which I would, as the CEO, have more than mere title in the organization, more than mere influence. I would in time become not just a major player in the organization, but the principal player and decision-maker.

And I would aspire to become something other than Machiavelli's Prince. I would aspire to become a leader of my own making, of my own imagination and experience and intellect. I would aspire to become after three decades of professional experience and of broadening and deepening a love of the liberal arts, the leader I hoped to one day be: the leader as liberal thinker.

Epilogue

Excess and defect are characteristic of vice,
and the mean of virtue; For men are good
in one way and bad in many.
~Aristotle

For what is more agreeable than wisdom itself
when thou thinkest of the security and the happy course
of all things which depend on the faculty
of understanding and knowledge.
~Marcus Aurelius

The Leader as Liberal Thinker

Our great and glorious masterpiece
is to live appropriately.
~Montaigne

I was thinking about the final stages of this story one afternoon and how I could sum up this "sundry life and uncertain times," when I received a phone call from an old friend who had stunning news to tell me. Julie Cummings and I have been friends since the early eighties, and it is not unusual to get an occasional call from her.

We had had a couple of conversations recently about our national organization opening two new executive vice president positions, a move we both saw as an attempt to find the eventual successor to the international president Eileen Boyer.

Julie Cummings knew what my position was on Eileen's successor: that Julie herself, because of her experience and success as the CEO of four major Youth Association organizations in a distinguished twenty-five year career, was ideally suited to succeed Eileen. Julie's other attributes made the case even more compelling: she was smart, tough, well-educated; she was now in her early fifties, an age by which Plato and Confucius believed that wisdom would come; and she was an attractive and charming Southerner from uptown New Orleans who could schmooze the philanthropic class and the political class as adroitly as any college president. No one, it seems, is ever perfect for a particular position, but Julie Cummings was for me as close as it gets to being perfect for the national president position.

But perhaps it was this very idea of perfection that unraveled what I had envisaged for her, because in explaining to me why she had been asked to resign from her CEO position that afternoon, the only reason Julie could summon was that she had on principle insisted that staff perform the jobs they were hired to perform and that they perform them consistently and competently. Toppling a sitting CEO almost always begins with disaffected staff, but Julie Cummings's circumstances were complicated by the fact that the organization was also trying to initiate a succession plan, the centerpiece of which was the hiring—by the board, not by Julie—of a chief operating officer. The succession plan empowered an executive committee of the board to meet without the CEO present to interview and hire a COO, who would then report to Julie but also be positioned to succeed her. Nonprofit CEOs certainly need a second-in-command, but one that they, not the board, chooses.

Julie could have contested the executive committee's request that she resign—there was at this point no formal approval by the full board—but she decided to accept a severance package and start her own consulting business instead. So here was someone I had envisaged as the next international president of our organization, someone of considerable ability, experience and executive accomplishment, suddenly dismissed from a local organization because she was perhaps too tough in her expectations of staff. I was understandably stunned, but upon reflection, not at all surprised. My friend Julie's difficulties, like my own, are emblematic of one of the overarching themes of this narrative: that even when one is succeeding, the vicissitudes of survival lay in waiting; and even when one's performance is incandescently good, it can be clouded and corrupted by political machinations. Inherent in the political dimension of nonprofits is the idea, beautifully expressed by the novelist Marguerite Yourcenar, that "catastrophe and ruin will come; disorder will triumph, but order will too, from time to time."

In time, order did indeed return for me, but not before the political machinery of the institution, particularly the board development and personnel decision-making machinery, came under my predominant influence, and not before those who once wielded that machinery—board members like DiTullio and Miller, Bolden and Schroeder, Santone and Hathaway—either disappeared into a corner of the community or departed for a stage more public and problematic.

Those who disappeared into a quiet corner of the community included Ed Bolden, who abruptly retired from his position as college coach. Curt Schroeder, after his wife died, practiced less law and spent more time at his favorite social club. Larry Miller never found the job he told the board of directors he wanted, but his name frequently appeared in the newspaper—usually with about twenty other people—in recognition for having solved a riddle posed by the paper.

Connie Santone and Bobby Hathaway stepped onto the political stage, engineering the election of a bright but brash young lawyer and city councilman to mayor of the city. It turned out to be one of the most tumultuous mayoral terms in the history of Erie politics. For about halfway into the mayor's four-year term, the mayor and Bobby Hathaway were indicted on felony charges which alleged that they had used inside information to buy up property near a site they themselves supposedly supported for the construction of a casino. They were both acquitted at trial, but the pressure and publicity surrounding it caused the collapse of their administration, its only accomplishment being the beleaguered but respected performance of Connie Santone as the mayor's top assistant and surrogate.

Then there was the man whose political acumen aligned this group against me, a seemingly uncomplicated man who was nothing short of brilliant as a grassroots politician, the inimitable Tommy DiTullio. Although Tommy remained on the board at Denny Maloney's request, he never attended another meeting. His health failed precipitously: heart failure, dialysis, stroke—all of it culminating in a hospital bed death watch. Denny suggested I visit Tommy. His suggestion hinted not at the fulfillment of a social obligation but at healing and reconciliation. I went, but with doubts about what I might find there, and deeper doubts about reaching any reconciliation with Tommy. I was not sure what, if anything, we would have to say to each other.

When I walked into his hospital room, I was surprised to see no one other than Tommy there. He lay in bed, half propped up, his full head of silver hair looking as impeccable as it had always looked, but his olive skin tinted yellow from the debilitating dialysis. I asked him how he was, and for a moment the old Tommy returned, the one who had been like a brother to me. His eyes—and Tommy had the biggest, most protuberant brown eyes I had ever seen—rolled around in good-natured disregard for his circumstances. His smile had the mischievous look of a man oddly pleased with his own predicament, however difficult it was. But the happy moment quickly passed, and his eyes suddenly glistened with melancholy rather than mischief. He tried to talk, but only a croak came out, and he fell silent. I stood at the side of his bed. I noticed that his right hand, which had lain limp at his side, was now opened and raised up slightly. Tommy was offering me his hand. He wanted to forgive, and perhaps forget, what had come between us. I took his hand and held it, and though no words were spoken, what this moment meant was quite clear to me. It meant that the unpleasantness that had come between us had been forgiven, but not for me, forgotten. I would always remember, however unpleasant it was to do so, the life lessons I learned from that masterful but mischievous politician.

It would take me more than a year to find my footing again in community life. Tommy Di-

Tullio, once our town's most conspicuous citizen, a man I had often described to others as never having met a single soul he did not know, had made my introduction to the community so ubiquitous that I had begun to see myself as the city's second citizen. I went everywhere with Tommy in those early years. I went to political fundraisers and charity balls, to public meetings and social clubs, to lectures, parties, communion breakfasts, and to testimonial dinners. I even went to funeral parlors with Tommy to see the dead I did not know and to express my condolences to family members I had never met. I went everywhere with Tommy, everywhere a new introduction could be made or an old community connection solidified. During those early years, I had by my own inclination and by Tommy's encouragement the initiative to, among other things, serve on the city's bicentennial commission, chair my Rotary Agency's foundation, and co-chair a capital campaign at my church. My community presence became so pervasive that powerful people with a political stake in the community suggested to Tommy that I become a candidate for mayor.

But after the failed attempt to topple me, I withdrew from community life. I mistakenly believed a largely private matter that had played itself out in the smaller confines of my own organization had penetrated the public's consciousness. I mistakenly believed that everyone I now encountered would have reservations about my personal and professional integrity. Having forgotten the lessons I learned from Stoics like Seneca and Marcus Aurelius, lessons I would revisit in the aftermath of this personal and professional crisis, I was for a time ashamed of what I thought others might be thinking of me. Later, as I reentered community life—though never with the same salience I had enjoyed under the tutelage of the Everyman DiTullio—I did so with the renewed understanding that there were things I could not control, and my reputation was one of them. What I could control, as demonstrated to me by the political genius of Tommy DiTullio, were the political dynamics of my own organization.

I say "my own" organization because the idea of organizational ownership was one of the fundamental lessons Tommy taught me. For Tommy, the fact that one was employed as the CEO of an organization did not confer on one any real authority or leadership. Not even a deep dedication to the institution conferred such authority. For him, authority, or leadership, came from political mastery, and political mastery flowed from the idea—the presumption really—that CEOs see themselves not as employees of nonprofit institutions, but as owners. "You have to take ownership," he said. "You have to believe that you own the place." Without this proprietary view, some of the executive actions required to exercise strong leadership, like taking command of the power of appointment to the board and managing committees, succession and the Machiavellians in one's midst—might otherwise be left to others: to the discretion of ambitious board members, to the maneuverings of disaffected staff, or to the vagaries of consensus decision-making. "You have to see yourself," Tommy said, "as numero uno."

But CEOs who come to see themselves in this proprietary light, as owners of the institution, as the number one leader of the enterprise, can also come to grief not by politics but by hubris, by the sometimes outrageous arrogance and pride that accompany political mastery. That was one of the fundamental lessons I came to realize after being knocked back by the coup that nearly toppled me. Even if one's vision is so ambitiously overconfident that, from the viewpoint of antiquity, it invites the displeasure of the gods; even if one's political acumen is so unrivaled that success seems to come without effort—it is wise to remember that the overconfident are almost always undone by a backlash of resentment. This does not mean that overconfidence ought to be disguised by false humility. It means that the passion of overconfidence needs to be rationally set aside in favor of Aristotle's mean of modesty, which is that true point of excellence between humility and pride. But the mean of modesty, as important as it is, cannot pervade a leader's sense of self without a dispassionate temperament to match it. This is what is so remarkable about the political figure Barack Obama, a relatively young man with the poise and equanimity of an old sage.

Reflecting on my own experience, it would seem that an unflappable temperament of the kind that Obama instinctively displays can be learned or at least rationally controlled. For me the age of fifty was the watershed. Prior to turning fifty I had a tendency to get "riled," to use Brian Billingsley's description, and to display a public passion that lacked proportion. After fifty, the public passion subsided. Was it simply a matter of having gotten older? The notable example of public passion by an older man like John McCain seems to suggest another explanation. Maybe my equilibrium of temperament was forged in the unhappiness brought down on me by the political machinations of my old friend Tommy DiTullio. Or maybe my heart attack, which prompted me to reflect on my own mortality and on the mortality of humanity in general, made me more appreciative of life's simple wisdom than of its passionate insight. Whether in the crucible of my own personal and professional experiences or in the reading and reflection of a theoretical life only my family and a few friends are privy to, I have come to admire those who become what Allan Bloom called a people of taste: citizens who have thought deeply about life's larger meaning and who have sought a "natural harmony between (their) passions and (their) knowledge." Or more grandly put, in the words of Marguerite Yourcenar, I have come to admire those who read and reflect, and in their best moments rise above the human.

Unfortunately, a lack of intellectual interest in life's larger meaning has produced vulgar mediocrities even at the very highest levels of American life. In the average nonprofit, particularly in smaller community agencies like my own, this lack of curiosity about the meaning of life is as pervasive as it is among the young in our colleges and universities. Anthony Kronman, the former Dean of the Yale Law School, has rightly observed of today's college students: "That a life is a career is for them an article of faith." What Kronman could have said had he been looking at a broader spectrum of Americans is that virtually every living generation today has either made the idea of a career central to a fulfilling life or has divorced it from any connection to life as a whole. For Kronman, "a career—any career—has a horizon narrower than that of the life of the person whose career it is." A career, for it to have its fullest meaning, must be placed in the context of a life lived well, a life in which the professional converges with the personal, the enviable with the admirable, the self with family, friends, community, country, humanity. A career, seen as the smaller circle within the larger circle of life, needs to be so placed not to make people better at their jobs—though it may in fact do just that, at least ethically and intellectually—but to make them better at being human.

And it is this very idea of being good at being human that no longer commands our attention, not even where one would expect to find it a central preoccupation, in colleges and universities. There the students are all careerists, the faculty research scientists or some other kind of "ist" like feminist or deconstructionist, and the administrators marketers and money-makers and builders of billion-dollar endowments. The liberal arts or humanities, which Kronman calls "education in the art of living," has declined precipitously in importance, while the sciences, and to a lesser extent the social sciences, have become preeminent on college and university campuses. Our preoccupation with the potency of science and technology, as Kronman has so eloquently argued, has diverted higher education from its now forgotten emphasis on the humanities and from its once historic mission of providing education in the meaning of life—an education now sorely needed for all undergraduates, but especially those expected to lead the major institutions of our nation, and especially those expected to lead nonprofit institutions like my own.

And if higher education, enamored as it is by scientific research and political correctness, is inhospitable to the idea of a liberal education, an education in which, as Allan Bloom believed, students ought to be taught to be adept at reflection of the broadest and deepest kind, then the business community in which nonprofit CEOs operate can understandably be expected to be even less hospitable. Even a business thinker like Peter Drucker, whose breadth and depth of learning are on display in almost everything he has written, is at best dubious about the modern merits of a liberal education. He is willing to concede that we should not entirely repudiate the wisdom of the past, but he is also convinced that a knowledge of the past can neither command the present nor mold the future. What Drucker believes the knowledge society needs are leaders who can understand and integrate a global society of disparate knowledges. Drawing on his knowledge of literature, Drucker cites Hermann Hesse's novel **The Glass Bead Game** as further testimony to the limitations of the liberal arts tradition. In Hesse's novel the hero leaves a utopian community of intellectuals dedicated to the wisdom of the past and returns to the vulgarity of everyday reality, because, as Drucker sees it, "his values are only fool's gold unless they have relevance to the world." So here we have one of the great gurus of business literature relying on a work of imaginative literature to point out that the literature of the past, the antiquated tradition of the humanities, has no relevance to the modern world. Here we have a business writer whose doubts about the liberal tradition of higher education, in a work called **The Essential Drucker**, referring to a line-up of intellectuals so long that it could comprise its own bibliography for a liberal arts education. There in **The Essential Drucker** are Archimedes and Alexander, Beethoven and Bismarck, Caesar, Darwin, Descartes, Dickens and Disraeli, Einstein and Engels, Goethe and Galileo, Jefferson, Kant, Leibniz, da Vinci, Lincoln, Mao, Marx and Moliere, Nietzsche, Planck and Plato, Adam Smith and Alexis de Tocqueville, Whitehead and Wittgenstein.

Despite all his liberal learning, Drucker can be bluntly dismissive of a liberal education. "Their liberal education," he writes, "does not enable them to understand reality, let alone master it." Perhaps Drucker thinks that a liberal education is appropriate for a writer, even a business writer, but not for being the CEO of a business or nonprofit. My own experience—personally, professionally, and intellectually—tells me that public policy thinkers like Charles Murray are right when they argue that those who lead at the highest levels of our society need an education that will "make them into wiser adults." What our leaders and future leaders need to know, in Murray's view, is "what good means—good as it applies to virtue, and the Good as a way of thinking about how to live a human life." This is the same thing that the leaders of our smaller institutions, of community agencies like my own, need to know. They need to know, as Frances Hesselbein succinctly said, how to be. In knowing how to be, they can then become the leader as liberal thinker—not liberal in the political context of the early 21st century, but liberal in the classical sense of a leader living a life of the mind combined with a life of virtue.

Even if you are not nearly the kind of liberal leader I have described and, therefore, feel completely unprepared to pursue its path, do not for a moment think that it cannot be done. It can most certainly be done. Even those of us who received some grounding in the liberal arts as undergraduate students (what we actually received were the inchoate vestiges of a once noble tradition that has, as Anthony Kronman observed, declined into relative obscurity), we entered into our careers poorly prepared to think about a career in the context of a meaningful life. Even if we had had an extraordinarily profound and well integrated undergraduate education in the humanities, we would have come into the world and into our careers and into our adult lives with only the barest blueprint as to how to live it. Filling in that blueprint, with our personal and professional experiences, with the breadth of our reading and the depth of our reflections, with the practice of virtues as old as antiquity (courage of conviction, modesty, moderation, truth and fairness), can, if we are lucky, and if we are persistent, lead to the kind of wisdom that Plato said comes with age. And any time in our lives is as good as any other to begin this journey of personal and professional and intellectual discovery. Begun when young, the task takes a lifetime. Begun later, after the knowledge that comes simply from living one's life, the length of the journey shortens but its profundity does not.

But where to begin anew the good life, the life of the leader as liberal thinker, when one has already begun, when one is already well into the journey? The bibliography of this book is one blueprint, limited as it is. Gladstone, one of Great Britain's greatest leaders, thought his alma mater Oxford ought to prepare the nation's future leaders by having their entire undergraduate experience consist of the study of only two works of literature, Homer's **Iliad** and **Odyssey**. My two works—and I only suggest them as a beginning point—are at opposite ends of the ethical spectrum: the **Meditations** of Marcus Aurelius and Machiavelli's **The Prince,** Aurelius for his wise counsel in the art of human goodness, Machiavelli for his cold-hearted but clear dissection of the political propensities of human nature, Aurelius for the good in mankind, Machiavelli for the evil.

This dichotomy between what is good and what is not in human nature is the great ethical conundrum of our age or any other age. It is a key conundrum of humanity and of leaders at all levels of society, including of course the ever growing number of CEOs of nonprofit institutions. Machiavelli's resolution to this quandary was simple: be good when you can; enter into evil when you must. Aurelius would have one be benevolent to the unjust. I cannot resolve this dichotomy. Perhaps science, in its hubris, will engineer this dichotomy out of existence by remaking humanity. Otherwise Desmond MacCarthy's estimate of humanity—that "society changes quickly; the soul hardly at all"—will probably continue to prevail. In the interim, I can only offer this: leaders can command the political machinery of any institution without entering into the dark world that Machiavelli described. They can do it, as the American essayist Joseph Epstein wrote of the English aphorist Sydney Smith, by becoming "one of those altogether agreeable men who absolutely know their own worth and (who) was, consistent with his desire to remain agreeable, not to be pushed around, taken advantage of, or otherwise trifled with."

In the future that Frances Hesselbein envisioned, the greatest of our nonprofit CEOs will not necessarily be great at strategy (vision) or tactics (analysis) or even leadership itself (idea development and inspiration). They will instead be great at being human, at what Desmond MacCarthy called "superior humanity." And their art will be, as Marcus Aurelius wisely observed, to be good.

Acknowledgements

In the solitude of composing a book, writers are understandably lulled into perceiving their works as wholly, singularly, indisputably theirs. But books are never really the work of one writer, one intellect. Their works are not simply theirs, just as this book, The Nonprofit Leader as Liberal Thinker, is not simply mine. It is the work of three decades of experience in the realm of nonprofit leadership and management and an even greater period of sustained reading and reflection in disciplines ranging from history and literature and business to science and philosophy. But mostly it is the work of an exchange of ideas with family, friends and colleagues.

Family members who have influenced this book both directly and indirectly are my wife Jan, who is wiser than I ever will be, my daughter Alyssa, whose blithe spirit has always been an inspiration, my granddaughters Halle and Leah, who are reminders of what talent and charisma look like, and finally my daughter Denise, without whose intelligence, tenacity and loyalty I would not have survived—professionally or personally—the events described in this book.

Friends who read the book in manuscript and offered valuable criticism to improve it are George Blakeslee, Tom Vinca, Linda King, Rick Lamb, Dr. Ken Schiff, and Dr. Kathleen Noce. George Blakeslee was the first to encourage me to write the Nonprofit Leader and Ken Schiff's editorial eye made the book much better structurally and stylistically. Bev Verbeke and Kathy Noce were invaluable in getting the book revised and formatted for publication.

Friends and colleagues who made significant contributions to this book include my good friend and colleague John Popoff, Mark Wassell, Jeff Szumigale, Vinnie Marchant, Michael Deluca, Len Ekimoff, Dr.George D'Angelo, Dr. Dick Rahner, Kate Strosser, Bruce Whitehair, Bill Bleil, Owen McCormick, Dr. Jim Barker, Michael Murawsky, Carl Carlotti, Dr. Bob Oliver, Nancy Taylor, Joe Grucza, Joe Grogan, John Flanagan, and Anne Stern.

Many of the ideas in this book were forged and tested in discussions with colleagues from two executive leadership groups. In each case I gained more than I gave to my colleagues in these groups. To the leadership group I founded, I am indebted to Karen Moski, Linda King,

Tyco Swick, Tom Vinca, Mike Murnock, Cheryl Koble, Lynn Begue, John Furhmann and Patricia Smith. To the Princeton Crew, for which I serve as chairman, I owe a debt to Jeff Palmer, George Krupanski, Joe Lynch, Bill Parks, Stan Pittman, Jack Ribas, Dave Ross, Brian Skanes, Peter Thornton, Russell Triolo, Jeff Waldron, Mary Ellen Kiernan, and my long-time friend and mentor, Bob Kiernan.

Others notable for their friendship with and influence on me are my brother Gary Messina, my cousin Dennis Cerami, my brother-in-law Joel Hart, Tony Annunziato, Robbie Callaway, Roxanne Spillett, Debbie Verges, Jim Caufield, Bob Parks, and another long-time friend and intellectual mentor, Dr. Bill Garvey; and finally two friends and colleagues who left this world of appearances for one that I trust is more metaphysically substantial: Tom Smart and Bruce Thompson.

Bibliography

Aristotle. "Nichomachean Ethics" translated by W.D. Ross and "Politics" translated by Benjamin Jowett. In The Basic Works of Aristotle. Edited by Richard McKeon. New York: Random House, 1941.

Aurelius, Marcus. Meditations. Translated by George Long. New York: Barnes & Noble, Inc., 2003.

Bebbington, David W. The Mind of Gladstone: Religion, Homer, and Politics. New York: Oxford University Press, 2004.

Berlin, Isaiah. The Hedgehog and the Fox. Chicago: Elephant Paperbacks, 1993.

Bloom, Allan. The Closing of the American Mind. New York: Simon and Schuster, 1987.

Bloom, Allan with Jaffa, Harry V. Shakespeare's Politics. Chicago: University of Chicago Press, 1964.

Carlson, Mim and Donohue, Margaret. The Executive Director's Survival Guide. San Francisco: Jossey-Bass, 2003.

Churchill, Winston S. History of the English Speaking Peoples. Edited by Henry Steele Commager. New York: Barnes & Noble Books, 1995.

Cicero, Marcus Tullius. On Moral Ends. Edited by Julia Annas and translated by Raphael Woolf. Cambridge: Cambridge University Press, 2001.

Coleridge, Samuel Taylor. "Selections from Biographia Literaria." In Criticism: The Major Statements. Selected and Edited by Charles Kaplan. New York: St. Martin's Press, 1975.

Collins, James C. and Porras, Jerry I. Built to Last. New York: HarperBusiness, 1997.

Collins, Jim. Good to Great. New York: HarperBusiness, 2001.

______. Good to Great and the Social Sectors. A Monograph to Accompany Good to Great. Boulder: 2005.

Drucker, Peter. The Essential Drucker. New York: HarperCollins, 2001.

Epictetus. Encheiridion. Translated by George Long. New York: Barnes & Noble, Inc., 2005.

Epstein, Joseph. "The Mere Common Sense of Sydney Smith" and "Desmond MacCarthy's Familiar Criticism." In Pertinent Players. New York: W.W. Norton & Company, 1993.

Friedman, Thomas L. The World Is Flat. New York: Farrar, Straus and Giroux, 2005.

Greene, Brian. The Fabric of the Cosmos. New York: Alfred A. Knopf, 2004.

Gunther, John. Death Be Not Proud. New York: Harper & Row, 1949.

Hamburg, Beatrix A. and David A. Learning To Live Together. New York: Oxford University Press, 2004.

Kant, Immanuel. Foundations of the Metaphysics of Morals. Translated by Lewis White Beck. New York: Prentice Hall, 1989.

Kronman, Anthony. Education's End. New Haven: Yale University Press, 2007.

La Rochefoucauld, Francois. Maxims. Translated by Leonard Tancock. New York: Penquin Books, 1959.

Machiavelli, Niccolo. Discourses on Livy. Translated by Harvey C. Mansfield and Nathan Tarcov. Chicago: University of Chicago Press, 1998.

______. The Prince. Translated by Luigi Ricci and revised by E.R.P. Vincent. New York: New American Library, 1952.

MacIntyre, Alasdair. After Virtue. Notre Dame: University of Notre Dame Press, 1984.

Mansfield, Harvey C. Machiavelli's Virtue. Chicago: University of Chicago Press, 1996.

Mill, John Stuart. Utilitarianism. Edited by George Sher. Indianapolis: Hacket Publishing Company, 2002.

Mintzberg, Henry. The Rise and Fall of Strategic Planning. New York: The Free Press, 1994.

Montaigne. The Complete Essays. Translated by Donald M. Frame. Stanford: Stanford University Press, 1965.

Munroe, Eleanor, Selections and Introduction. Readings for Remembrance. New York: Penquin Books, 2000.

Murray, Charles. Real Education. New York: Crown Forum, 2008.

Nozick, Robert. The Examined Life. New York: Simon & Schuster, 1989.

Nuland, Sherwin B. How We Die. New York: Random House, 1993.

Plato. Philebus. Translated by Benjamin Jowett. Fairford: Echo Library, 2006.

______. The Republic of Plato. Translated by Francis MacDonald Cornford. New York: Oxford University Press, 1968.

Ridley, Jasper Godwin. Lord Palmerston. New York: Dutton, 1971.

Ross, W.D. The Right and the Good. Edited by Philip Stratton-Lake. Oxford: Oxford University Press, 1930.

Rossiter, Clinton, ed. The Federalist Papers. New York: New American Library, 2003.

Seneca. Moral and Political Essays. Edited by John M. Cooper and translated by J.F. Procope. New York: Cambridge University Press, 1995.

Shakespeare, William. "Julius Caesar" and "Othello, The Moor of Venice." In The Complete Works of William Shakespeare. New York: Avenel Books, 1975.

Sun-tzu. The Art of War. Translated by Ralph D. Sawyer. Boulder: Westview Press, 1994.

Swift, Jonathan. Gulliver's Travels. New York: Barnes & Noble Classics, 2003.

Williams, John. Augustus. New York: Vintage International, 2004.

Yourcenar, Marguerite. Memoirs of Hadrian. New York: Farrar, Straus and Giroux, 1963.

Index

Index

Index

Made in United States
North Haven, CT
04 November 2026

21765282R00243